MW01257797

ALSO BY RANDY TURNER

NON-FICTION

5:41: Stories from the Joplin Tornado
(with John Hacker)

Silver Lining in a Funnel Cloud:
Greed, Corruption and the Joplin Tornado

Newton County Memories

Lost Angels: The Murders of Rowan Ford and Doug Ringler

Let Teachers Teach

Spirit of Hope: The Year After the Joplin Tornado
(with John Hacker)

Scars from the Tornado:
One Year at Joplin East Middle School

NOVELS

No Child Left Alive

Devil's Messenger

Small Town News

The

BUCK

STARTS

here!

Harry S. Truman and the City of Lamar

RANDY TURNER

For the City of Lamar- where legends are born and where often legends choose to remain

ACKNOWLEDGMENTS

The idea of writing a book about Harry Truman and Lamar is something that first occurred to me in 1984 and while I thought about it again from time to time, the idea of writing a book about Truman's connection to a town that he left when he was 10 months old did not seem to be one that was worth pursuing.

After all, Truman only returned to the city a handful of times and never for more than a few hours.

If there was a book in it, the first time period I needed to research was not the 1880s and the often told story about the arrival of mule trader John Anderson Truman and his wife Martha Ellen Young Truman to Lamar and the birth of their son, but August 31, 1944, when Truman returned to accept the vice presidential nomination.

I started researching into the events surrounding the 1944 Democratic National Convention to get a feel of the time and the events leading up to Truman's return.

Beginning my research by reviewing microfilm of the *Lamar Democrat* in the Barton County Historical Society, I discovered that during that time period Sheriff Roy Patterson

ACKNOWLEDGMENTS

and his son Sammie were murdered, a murder that harkened back to the murder of another Barton County Sheriff and his son 25 years earlier, Richard Chancellor was reported missing in action and Lamar had its second war casualty.

As I began reviewing other newspapers' coverage of Truman's visit, I began to grasp something I had never realized. Truman not only a delivered a speech on the west side of the Barton County Courthouse, he delivered a speech of historical importance.

With the nationwide radio hookup, it was not only the speech that launched the Democratic portion of the 1944 general election race, but it was the first major national speech for a man who a few months later became President of the United States.

After that, I had no doubts about writing this book.

Thanks to the microfilmed copies of the *Democrat* and Chad Stebbins' essential biography of Arthur Aull, I knew I would have no problem interweaving his story into the book.

I interviewed some of the people who have since passed on, including Richard Chancellor, Gerald Gilkey, Betty Aull White and Loyd Gathman, when I was an editor and reporter for the *Democrat* in the 1980s.

I also had the good fortune to work with Reba Earp Young, who shared many stories of the early days of Lamar. On one occasion, two Wyatt Earp experts came to Lamar for research on a book they were doing on the famed lawman. The experts did not impress me and to this day I have never been able to determine if they actually wrote the book, but I learned a lot from Reba about the Earp family that day.

Best of all, I was privileged to know and work with Marvin VanGilder.

ACKNOWLEDGMENTS

I first met Marvin in 1984 at the Truman Centennial, when I thanked him for his wonderful history *The Story of Barton County*. I used facts gleaned from that book, as well as the bound volumes of the *Democrat* from 1882 to 1884 and information provided to me by Nell Finley and Rita Embry at the Truman Birthplace when I wrote the Truman Pageant.

At the *Carthage Press* in the 1990s, I worked with and, more importantly, learned from Marvin much about the history of Carthage, Lamar and Barton County and listened to his recollections of the Truman 1959 visit, his conversations and correspondence with the former president and the night he interviewed both Truman and Thomas Hart Benton.

In 1996, *Carthage Press* Publisher Jim Farley asked me to come up with a plan for starting a weekly newspaper in Joplin. American Publishing, which owned the Press, vetoed the plan, but not long after that, Farley asked me if I could do a weekly for Lamar.

I may be the only person to still have every copy, all 49 of them, of the *Lamar Press*, which was launched August 15, 1996, as far as I can tell, without the approval of American Publishing.

The columns Marvin wrote for the *Lamar Press* were a valuable resource in the writing of this book.

Information for the 1800s portion of the book came from microfilmed copies of the *Lamar Democrat, Barton County Progress, Lamar Southwest Missourian* and some southeast Kansas newspapers that are mentioned when they are cited. Also biographies of Truman were consulted, all of which are listed in the bibliography.

Much of the information on the early career of Arthur Aull comes from the Chad Stebbins book and microfilmed copies of the *Democrat*.

Much information about Richard Chancellor and the Chancellor family came from a 2019 interview with Ione Chancellor, a first-person recollection of the first time he was missing in action written for her after her husband's death by bombardier Joe Young and an unfinished manuscript by Chancellor detailing how he got into the service and how he met his future wife.

A brief history of Richard Chancellor and his family written by Ione Chancellor and given to the Barton County Historical Society provided a great deal of information as well as *Democrat* articles from 1944 and 1945 and interviews Chancellor did latter with Mike Surbrugg of the *Joplin Globe* in 1977 and with me in the '80s. I also received information about Chancellor in my interviews with Nell Finley and Hannah Oeltjen, as well as from census records and military records from the National Archives.

For the portions of the book dealing with Gerald Gilkey, sources included my interviews with Betty Gilkey, Steve Gilkey, Nancy Gilkey, Courtney Gardner, Katie Gilkey, Carolyn Taffner, Traci Cox, Hannah Oeltjen, Ione Chancellor and Kent Harris, interviews I did with him during the 1980s and 1990s, a book compiled by city staff and given to him when he retired in 2001, census records and military records. Information on the unveiling of the Gilkey portrait in 2006 comes from my coverage on my blog the *Turner Report*.

In addition to the *Democrat* and Truman biographies, sources for the story of Truman's 1944 visit included coverage from the *New York Times*, the *Joplin Globe*, *Joplin News-Herald*, Associated Press, United Press, materials from the Truman Library, including a descriptive oral history from Gerald

Ione and Richard Chancellor. *Photo courtesy of Ione Chancellor*

Reinsch about preparing Truman for the speech. The Truman Birthplace also provided me with an opportunity to watch the film of Truman's speech, which provided me with details about the people who were attending, as well as Truman's gestures and points of emphasis. I also received information from my interviews with Louise Caruthers and Hannah Oeltjen and from an interview I did with Loyd Gathman in 1984.

When writing about people who are gifted in their use of the English language, including Arthur Aull, Madeleine Aull VanHafften, Lee Chiswell and Harry Truman, I tried as often as possible to let them use their own words and get out of the way.

I used the same approach with Marvin VanGilder. When I worked at the *Lamar Democrat* in the 1980s, I was taken by the enormous respect people had for Marvin, something I attributed to his authorship of *The Story of Barton County* and his status as a Barton County native.

I developed a greater understanding after working with him and in his descriptions of the *Lamar Journal* from his *Lamar Press* columns, but I never understood just how important he was in the history of Lamar journalism until I received a treasure trove of information from his son, Chris VanGilder, in the summer of 2019, including some of his work for the *Journal*.

Frances Cato was an invaluable source of information about her uncle and father, Brother and B. B. Adams, and their trip to the nation's capital for the inauguration in 1949, as was the *Democrat* and the Joplin, St. Louis and Kansas City newspapers.

Reba Young's book provided a valuable resource on her family, the Earps, as did Marvin VanGilder's recounting of his step-grandmother's story of how Wyatt Earp was run out of Lamar.

Sources for Truman's 1959 return include the *Carthage Press*, *Joplin Globe*, *Joplin News-Herald*, *New York Times*, wire service accounts, the Truman Library, Truman Birthplace and interviews with Kent Harris, Louise Caruthers, Hannah Oeljen, Albert McManis, Justine McManis and my 1980s interview with Loyd Gathman.

Ione Chancellor, Hannah Oeltjen, the Barton County Historical Society and writings by Joe Davis of the Historical Society and Reba Young were valuable sources of information about the Travelers Hotel.

Information on Madeleine and Stan and Betty White, in addition to the Stebbins biography, came from an interview with Dorothy Parks, interviews I conducted years ago with Dorothy, Betty White, Lou Nell Bath and Opal Sims and personal recollections of stories told to me in the 1980s by Dorothy, Lou Nell, Opal and Russell Pierson and in the 1990s by Marvin VanGilder.

One of the drawbacks of writing a non-fiction work of this nature is the necessity of eliminating some fascinating historical information because it does not fit in with the rest of the book.

One such story was Lee Chiswell's article on a Baptist evangelist who came to preach in Lamar and tried to have his way with a minister's daughter. His recounting of the tale was hilarious, but in the end was a distraction to the story I was telling.

Another story that is not included, but shows how connected the lives of these people were is one I came across during my final interview for the book.

It was conducted at the house at 400 W. 11th where the Arthur Aull family lived for more than half a century. Joe Davis of the Barton County Historical Society provided an excellent history of this house in a recent *Lamar Democrat* article.

When the owner and her fiancée moved into the house, they brought with them an antique desk that her grandfather had purchased from its owner and kept at his place of business for years until the business closed.

Madeleine sold the desk, one that was used by her father, Arthur Aull, to the businessman not long before her death.

Now the desk has returned to its original home, thanks to Katie Gilkey and the foresight of her grandfather Gerald Gilkey.

At the front of the desk displayed prominently is another symbol of Lamar, a souvenir obtained during a trip to Independence with the message "The Buck Stops Here."

ACKNOWLEDGMENTS

Katie Gilkey, granddaughter of long time Lamar Mayor Gerald Gilkey, sits behind a desk once owned by Lamar Democrat Publisher Arthur Aull.

The book would not have been possible without the help from the folks at the Barton County Historical Society, the Truman Birthplace, the *Lamar Democrat*, the City of Lamar, the Carthage Public Library, the Jasper County Archives and Record Center, the Joplin Public Library and the Truman Library and Museum.

A special thanks to Chad Stebbins for sending me some of his Arthur Aull research and Chris VanGilder, who provided me with copies of some of his father's early work on *The Story of Barton County*, as well as clippings from the *Lamar Journal*.

I talked to or received help from a number of people while doing the research for the book, some of whom are quoted in these pages, all of whom offered valuable information or assistance.

Among those people were the following:

ACKNOWLEDGMENTS

A memorial stands on the west side of the Barton County Courthouse where Sen. Harry S. Truman gave his vice presidential acceptance speech on August 31, 1944. *Photo by Randy Turner*

Bev Baker, Beth Bazal, Beth Brisbin, Michelle Brooks, Carol Calton, Louise Caruthers, Frances Cato, Ione Chancellor, Traci Cox, Kristina Crockett, Joe Davis, Mike Davis, Jim Felts, Astra Ferris, Nell Finley, Courtney Gardner, Betty Gilkey, John Gilkey, Katie Gilkey, Kent Harris, Kay Hicks, Patty McKay, Albert McManis, Justine McManis, Melody Metzger, Sharon Nelson, Hannah Oeltjen, Dorothy Parks, Ben Reed, Mike Short, Chad Stebbins, Billy Strong, Willis Strong, Carolyn Taffner, Jeff Tucker, Chris VanGilder, Richard Walker and Julie Yokley

Photos of Harry S Truman are provided courtesy of the Truman Library and Museum. Photos were also provided by the Barton County Historical Society, the Gilkey family, Ione Chancellor and the Truman Birthplace.

INTRODUCTION

Jim Allen was tired of the City of Lamar, Missouri being considered an afterthought when newspaper reporters and historians told the story of its most famous native son—the 33rd President of the United States Harry S. Truman.

As the calendar year turned from 1983 to 1984, Allen who had helped turn Thorco into a nationally recognized business, was retired, but remained active in the community.

When the Lamar Chamber of Commerce asked him to spearhead its committee to plan the city's celebration of Truman's 100th birthday, he immediately accepted.

It grated Allen and many other Lamar residents that it seemed accepted that Truman was born in Independence, Missouri, and even Grandview where he had spent much of his youth, had laid claim to the Truman heritage.

Lamar- not so much.

It was in a two-story white frame house four blocks east of the square that Martha Ellen Young Truman gave birth to the future president on May 8, 1884.

Now that the 100th anniversary of that birth was going to be celebrated, Allen had a plan to shift the nation's attention to this community of 4,000.

At the first meeting of the Truman Centennial Committee, Allen laid out an ambitious goal that caught most of those in attendance by surprise.

"We have sent a letter to the White House asking President Reagan to come to Lamar."

The choice of the Republican commander-in-chief (though Reagan was still a Democrat when Truman was president) was surprising, but no one voiced any objections, as far as committee member Jim Felts recalls.

No one expressed any doubts that the President of the United States would agree to come to Lamar. Part of that was due to Jim Allen's long track record of success.

Allen, a silver-haired, bespectacled man in his '60s, bore a resemblance to Truman and projected an air of confidence and an easy command of the room.

And while Truman had little use for Republicans when he was alive, there was no doubt he would have enjoyed the irony of a Republican president traveling to the town where he was born to sing his praises.

Having the current President of the United States as the featured speaker would draw the nation's attention to Lamar and perhaps cement the city's claim to fame- not just as a one-sentence mention in encyclopedias, but also as a prominent feature in the biography of Harry S. Truman.

While the speaker was slated as the main event for the city's celebration, it was far from the only one. The American Legion was dedicating a monument at the Truman Birthplace and a Truman stamp cancellation was scheduled at the Lamar Post Office. A mule show celebrating the heritage of Truman's father, John Truman, was also on tap.

Music, games, a sidewalk sale and numerous other activities had been scheduled for Saturday, May 5, 1984.

A second major event, in addition to the keynote speaker, was planned for that day- a pageant celebrating Truman's birth.

The idea was originally conceived during a brainstorming session that included Nell Finley, Truman Birthplace curator Rita Embry, her assistant, and Genevieve Guinn, president of Lamar Community Betterment, among others.

Funding had been arranged through the Missouri Department of Natural Resources, which managed the historic site, and a pageant had been written, primarily using bound volumes of 1884 *Lamar Democrat* newspapers and information gathered by historian Marvin L. VanGilder and published in his book *The Story of Barton County.*

The pageant would tell the story of Lamar in 1884. Lamar Masonic Lodge members built a replica of storefronts that were on the square 100 years earlier. Lamar Art League members painted the sets.

Everyone from Mayor Gerald Gilkey, who had held that position for 19 years, to school age children participated as approximately 100 were cast in the Truman Pageant.

It took hundreds of hours of planning to get the City of Lamar ready for one of the biggest events in the city's existence.

Eventually, not only did President Reagan decline the invitation, but so did former President Jimmy Carter, former Vice President Walter Mondale and Sen. John Glenn. Finally, the committee convinced Missouri Lt. Gov. Ken Rothman, a Democratic candidate for governor, to come to Lamar.

"I was his Barton County campaign coordinator," Felts said.

The centennial celebration was designed to not only celebrate a man who had reached the pinnacle, but the city where it all began.

CHAPTER ONE

Though no one ever thought of Valerius Lee Chiswell, who wisely decided to go by his middle name, as a future president of the United States, those involved in Democratic politics in the State of Missouri saw a bright future ahead for the Barton County prosecuting attorney.

Like so many others in the years following the Civil War, Chiswell, who was born and spent his first two decades and studied law in Maryland, followed the famed newspaper editor Horace Greeley's motto of "Go west, young man" and decided that the City of Lamar, nestled in the southwestern corner of Missouri, would be the place where he would make his mark.

Chiswell opened a law office in the second floor of the Barton County Courthouse, where he would also serve as a collection agent.

In his advertisement in the *Barton County Southwest Missourian*, he promised "all business entrusted to his care will receive prompt attention."

It did not take long for Chiswell to climb the social and political ladders. He opened a law office on the town square and at the tender age of 24 in 1872 won a bitterly fought election to become prosecuting attorney.

It was during that election that Chiswell saw a glimpse of his future, though he probably did not realize it at the time. In those days of highly partisan newspapers, the *Barton County Southwest Missourian*, favoring his Republican opponent, took every scrap of negative information it could find about the young man, everything from Chiswell being "an Easterner" to aspersions on his character, often based on his courtroom tactics.

The *Southwest Missourian* attempted to twist Lee Chiswell's most striking positive qualities into negative ones. After all, how could you ever trust a lawyer who was tall, handsome, sported a meticulously groomed mustache and was always dressed in the finest clothes displaying a partiality for black, broadcloth coats?

Add to that, Chiswell's gift for soaring oratory and his ease with the written word and it was no wonder the Republican newspaper was skeptical about electing the young man to such an important position.

And of course, there was one negative aspect to Chiswell that disgusted the editor of the *Southwest Missourian* more than all of the others combined.

Lee Chiswell was a Democrat.

The attacks on Chiswell's character were relentless.

One such attack in the *Southwest Missourian* accused Chiswell of committing "little dirty chicanery" addressing him directly. "A trap baited with a gnat's gizzard would catch you and you know it and so does every person in the county."

Whether the people of Barton County knew of Chiswell's alleged chicanery, they did not seem to care.

Though Chiswell defeated his Republican opponent, he

never forgot the naked displays of partisanship the Republicans used in their efforts to derail his political ambitions.

Imagine what could be done if such an instrument were placed in the hands of someone who would use it for good, which to Chiswell meant a newspaper that could promote the Democratic Party.

As he began his first term as prosecuting attorney, the thought remained in the back of his mind. If someone knew what he was doing, a strong newspaper could serve as the voice of the people and make sure no Republicans were ever elected again in Barton County.

The Barton County government that Chiswell found himself a part of following his election as prosecuting attorney was not many years away from being a more typical frontier form of government.

It had only been a few years since Lamar officials decided it was time to bring law and order to the city.

It wasn't a rash of murders or burglaries that hastened a decision, but an onslaught of hogs roaming the streets.

In those days long before zoning, there was no dividing line between residential and agricultural and the livestock had a tendency to wander from its rightful home from time to time.

Unfortunately for those who were concerned about the effect hogs on the city streets was having on attracting new residents, a law is just a law if there is no one to enforce it and it wasn't until 1870 that Lamar finally hired a city marshal.

The new marshal, like Lee Chiswell, was someone who

came to Lamar to make his mark.

The Lamar City Council appointed young Wyatt Earp as the city's first marshal on March 3, 1870, just a year after he arrived, following other members of his family who had already settled in Lamar.

Being marshal provided steady employment for Earp, who turned 21 that month and was a newlywed, having married Urilla Sutherland at the Exchange Hotel, which was owned by her parents.

Earp's father, Nicholas Porter Earp, a justice of the peace, conducted the ceremony.

Earp and his bride lived at the Exchange Hotel for a while until he used his marshal's salary to buy a house for $56, a princely sum since his salary was only $15 a month.

With the hog problem seemingly a thing of the past, the biggest event of his brief time as marshal occurred in June 1870, when he arrested three drunken revelers at a local saloon.

One escaped the jail before morning and was not recaptured, while the other two were fined $5 for disturbing the peace.

After Earp's appointment, the council opted to make marshal an elected position and that November Earp squared off against his half-brother Newton Earp and was elected marshal with 137 votes to 108 for Newton.

Though Wyatt Earp became a name synonymous with frontier law, that was the only time Earp ever ran for office.

Shortly after Earp's election, Urilla Earp became ill and died at age 21 and it was not longer afterward that Wyatt Earp left Lamar for good.

It is not certain what caused him to leave. Some speculated it was grief over the loss of his beloved wife, while others were

Wyatt Earp, Lamar's first marshal.

just as convinced Wyatt Earp the lawman, was leaving just a step or two ahead of the law.

A Lamar woman named Amanda Cobb offered another version of Earp's departure.

At the time Earp was city marshal, Cobb was a teenage saloon girl at Elihu Martin's drinking establishment, which was frequented by Earp and his brothers and many other Lamar men who not only liked the atmosphere, but also enjoyed making advances at Cobb.

Shortly after Earp's wife Urilla died, members of her family who questioned the circumstances of her death, accosted Earp and his brothers at the saloon.

The man accused Earp of being responsible for Urilla's death. A barroom brawl broke out forcing Martin, who in addition to owning the establishment, served as bartender, bookkeeper and bouncer, to take action.

Martin kept numerous weapons under the bar in case any of his patrons caused problems, including a short-barreled, pearl-handled .32 caliber Smith & Wesson revolver

As the fight escalated, Martin reached under the bar, took out the .32 and fired it into the ceiling.

While that spared Martin's furniture, it did not stop the battle, which spilled out of the bar through the swinging doors and onto the north side of the square.

As a crowd gathered, the Earp brothers received a beating and were told to get out of town.

Whether that caused Wyatt Earp to leave Lamar forever will likely never be known.

Many members of the Earp family remained in Lamar and continued to play a key role in the city's history.

CHAPTER TWO

As the election of 1882 approached, Lee Chiswell had served 10 years as prosecuting attorney and was still a young man of 34.

With his gift for oratory, which he displayed during his courtroom appearances and at political meetings in Barton County and across the state, few doubted he was headed for statewide and perhaps even national political office.

Chiswell had other ideas.

At the 1882 Barton County Democratic Convention, Chiswell stunned the delegates when he declared he would not seek re-election.

There was an outcry from the Democrats who not only looked at Chiswell as a rising star who might bring prominence to Lamar and Barton County, but also as a sure bet to be re-elected and keep the office in Democratic hands.

An attempt was made to put Chiswell's name into nomination anyway, but he made it clear he had no intention of remaining prosecuting attorney.

While he reassured the delegates he would remain active in Democratic politics, he would concentrate on his legal practice and unspecified business interests.

Though Chiswell did not share his business plans with the delegates, he intended to enter a business that had never been far from his mind since his first political race a decade earlier.

Lamar was a thriving community and Chiswell planned to play an even more important role in its growth than he had during his political career.

Lamar's population had grown to 700, according to the 1880 census, and progressive city leaders worked to make the city welcoming and attractive.

The square was lined with elm and maple trees and the streets were covered with gravel, something Lamar did two years before the much larger city of Springfield followed suit.

Lamar had five churches- Baptist, Christian, Methodist, Presbyterian and Congregational and a thriving business community, complete with livery stables, real estate companies, banks and saloons.

The welcoming atmosphere of Lamar, an atmosphere that convinced people like Chiswell and the Earp family to put down roots, continued to attract others, including a young couple from the Grandview area.

John Anderson Truman, a 31-year-old mule and horse trader, and his wife Martha Ellen (Mattie) Young Truman, paid $685 to buy the Simon Blethrode place four blocks east of the square on Kentucky Avenue.

The Blethrode place was a corner lot measuring 80 by 150 feet. The small, white frame two-story house had six rooms, four downstairs and two upstairs.

The home had no basement, attic or clothes closet and the bathroom facilities, of course, were in a separate wooden building, constructed specifically for that purpose.

The deed was recorded at the Barton County Courthouse, November 14, 1882, but it would be six more months before Truman's name appeared in the newspaper.

The Trumans, who had been married a year, had moved to Lamar when Mrs. Truman was pregnant with what would have been their first child.

John and Martha Truman's first child was stillborn and is buried in Lake Cemetery, just west of the Lamar city limits. *Photo courtesy of Barton County Historical Society*

The child was stillborn on October 25, 1882.

Despite the sadness over losing a child, the Trumans decided they wanted to stay in Lamar.

There was no mention of the child in the newspaper. In 1882, newspapers served primarily as organs of political news, some local, much printed word for word from other publications, though always giving credit to the source newspapers.

And, of course, the advertising in the local newspaper kept the community informed on the services offered by bankers, real estate agents, doctors, lawyers and the new items in stock at local retail stores.

On the week the Trumans became landowners in Lamar, the major news was the sale at McCutchen, Jones & Company in the opera block on the south side of the square.

The proprietor, N. E. McCutchen, who was also Lamar's mayor, was offering "men's and ladies' underwear- the best it has ever been our pleasure to offer."

The ad for McCutchen's sale appeared on the pages of the *Barton County Progress*, a newspaper whose new owner fervently supported the Democratic Party.

Lee Chiswell and his law partner, Charles W. Huggins, were the new owners. Chiswell handled the editorial duties making it clear his political preferences and therefore, the newspaper's political preferences.

What should have been a crowning achievement for the Barton County Democratic Party, winning all but two county offices, county treasurer and county clerk, on November 7, 1882, was not good enough for Chiswell.

"Politics should not be a popularity contest," he wrote. "There are things which are of greater importance than the individual candidates. A person needs to vote for all the candidates of his party. Why else would you have parties?"

The Democratic candidates who were beaten should have won, Chiswell said and he blamed it on Republicans using the same methods they tried to use to defeat him in 1872.

"It seems to this casual observer that the heaping of abuse upon the heads of decent and honest men who become candidates for office is not the most successful manner of conducting a campaign."

Though Chiswell thoroughly enjoyed being a newspaper-man, he was never thrilled with his publication's name.

Legal complications kept him from discarding the *Barton County Progress* name immediately, but he had already decided on a new name for his newspaper.

While Chiswell was working to make his new venture a success, so was John Truman.

In addition to the $685 he paid for his home, Truman invested $200 in a barn across the street. It was there that he established his horse and mule trading business.

John Truman was a dreamer and 1883 was the year he was going to make those dreams become reality.

CHAPTER THREE

—— ∞ ——

Two events of major significance in Lamar occurred in May 1883, though only one was featured prominently in Lee Chiswell's newspaper.

As of May 17, 1883, the *Barton County Progress* ceased to exist and in its place was born the *Lamar Democrat*.

The news was trumpeted at the top of page one.

While Chiswell devoted several paragraphs to announce to readers there would be no doubt as to the political orientation of his publication, he paid only scant attention to another event that took place in Lamar.

The first graduation ceremonies for Lamar High School were held and the *Democrat* devoted one sentence to the event. No record exists of any of the parents of the five graduates complaining about the lack of attention.

John Truman took out an advertisement in the *Democrat* on June 20, 1883, in an effort to promote his struggling business.

"Mules bought and sold. I will keep for sale at the White Barn on Kentucky Avenue a lot of good mules. Anyone wanting teams will do well to call on J. A. Truman."

Truman worked from sunup to sunset to make a good life

for himself and his bride.

After the work was done, there were occasions when he attended political gatherings, since those served as the sporting events of the 1880s.

Truman was a Democrat tried and true, a trait he passed on to his sons. In his short time in Lamar, he had developed a reputation as a hard worker, an honest man and someone who was quick to defend his positions.

"My father was a fighter," Harry Truman said, "and if he didn't like what you did, he'd fight you."

That often put John Truman at a disadvantage since he stood only five feet six inches tall and weighed around 140 pounds. That did not stop him from battling anyone, his son said.

"He'd whip anybody up to 200 if they got in his way."

John Truman was not the only capable person living in that house on Kentucky Avenue.

As David McCulloch noted in his 1992 biography *Truman*, Martha Ellen Young "learned to bake, sew and use a rifle as well as a man."

Sunday meals, featuring Mattie's best dish, fried chicken, were a favorite at the Truman home.

The Trumans shared their home with John's sister, Mary Martha Truman and as they discovered in the late summer of 1883, they would soon have company.

A year and half after their first child was stillborn, John and Martha Truman learned they were getting a second chance at parenthood.

∞

As Lee Chiswell put his stamp on his newspaper, he entertained readers with a combination of political news, heavily favoring the Democratic Party, of course, and his whimsical musings on community news, describing somewhat personal events in detail.

In early May 1884, Chiswell wrote about a visitor to Lamar.

"Bill Moody is in town. It seems that he was asked to leave Appleton City and remain away 12 months. He married an overconfiding girl and then mistreated her.

"The girl's father clubbed him and finally shot at him. He was arrested and fined five dollars for not hitting him."

Chiswell reported on a "baby cyclone" that put a scare into Lamar residents May 7, 1884, but by the following day, the skies were clear and it was another typical day for the city.

That day's *Lamar Democrat* shows J. A. Albright advertising the "most complete stock of boots in southwest Missouri."

J. M. Fisher paid for "Prince, the Roadster Stallion, a beautiful bay with black points, six years old, 16 hands high and weighs 1,200 pounds of fine style and good action and is among the best bred stallions in the southwest."

The Palace Barber Shop and Bath Room promised "shaving, hair cutting and shampooing with ease and celerity" and promised satisfaction "or no charge."

Cunningham Drug Store offered the new miracle cure-Papillon Skin Care- "a specific cure for all skin diseases, salt rheum, rash, inflammation, insect bites, inordinate itching, ulcers, cuts, wounds, burns or scales and scrofulous eruptions (inflammation of the eyes and ears)."

Byrd's Ice Cream Parlor sought a different clientele, claiming to be "neat, clean and cozy," newly remodeled and claimed "it is the place to bring your girl."

In that day's newspaper, John Truman placed another advertisement.

"Wanted a few good mules and horses. Will pay highest cash prices for same. J. A. Truman, White Barn near Missouri Pacific Depot."

One thing that was not mentioned in the May 8, 1884 *Lamar Democrat* was another event that took place in Lamar that day. Births were not considered news at the *Democrat* even when the father was an advertiser.

Dr. William L. Griffin, who sported a distinguished thatch of white hair with a long, flowing beard to match, had established a successful practice in an office three blocks northeast of the square.

Griffin was a "physician, surgeon and obstetrician who paid special attention to chronic diseases and was an avid amateur historian.

Griffin was also $15 richer May 8, 1884, when he rode what he claimed to be "the fastest horse in Barton County" to the Truman home and delivered a baby for John and Martha in a downstairs room measuring six feet, six inches by 10 feet, nine inches.

Two days later, Martha Truman recalled years later, a Baptist circuit rider, Washington Pease, stopped by the Truman home, held tiny Harry aloft with the sun shining on the child and proclaimed what a sturdy baby he was.

On June 5, 1884, Griffin recorded on the birth certificate that a son was born May 8 along with the name and age of John and Martha Truman and John's occupation. The baby's name was not recorded for nearly six decades.

After his son was born, John Truman commemorated the occasion by planting a pine tree beside their home and legend

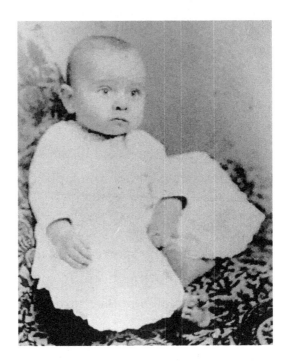

The only known baby picture of future president Harry Truman.
Photo courtesy of Truman Library and Museum

has it nailed a mule shoe above the door for good luck.

After debating what to call their son, John and Mattie elected to call him Harry after his uncle Harrison Young and gave him the middle initial "S" in honor of his grandfathers Solomon Young and Anderson Shippe Truman.

Harry S Truman spent the first 10 months of his life in Lamar, leaving the community too young to have any memories of it, only stories that were told to him by his parents.

With the mule business failing, John, Martha, and their infant son said goodbye to Lamar in March 1885, selling the home and the barn for $1,600 and moved to Harrisonville, Missouri.

It would be another 39 years before Harry Truman returned to the city where he was born.

CHAPTER FOUR

John and Mattie Truman's road took them first to Harri-sonville, then to Grandview and eventually to Independence, where they settled.

Though their imprint on Lamar's history would have been almost non-existent had they remained childless, the youngest member of the Truman clan (until the birth of his brother Vivian in 1886) would have an impact on Lamar that lasts to this day.

It would be a long time, however, before that impact began to be felt and Lamar's history continued to be written by those who remained behind after the Truman family headed upstate.

When the Trumans left in 1885, lawyer and fledgling news-paper editor Lee Chiswell continued to build his reputation in journalism and politics.

Still only 37, Chiswell's law practice was thriving, newspa-per circulation continued to grow and despite abandoning his role as prosecuting attorney, he was among less than a handful of people who held a firm grip on the Democratic party in Barton County.

His conversational tone in his columns, somewhat ahead

of its time, also garnered Chiswell followers among his fellow newspapermen in other communities who often reprinted his wry observations and colorful stories about life in Lamar.

Chiswell developed a certain celebrity in neighboring communities. His visit to Pittsburg, Kansas, 30 miles away, was noted in the *Pittsburg Democrat*.

"Lee Chiswell, the unterrified editor of the *Lamar Democrat*, called on Saturday evening," the newspaper's editor wrote.

Though Chiswell's musings were devoured by Missouri and Kansas editors eager to reprint them and attract readers, it was his use of the newspaper as a political platform that Chiswell used to improve his stock in state and national politics.

As he reached the age of 44 in 1892, the tall, dapper, impeccably dressed Chiswell delivered a stem-winding speech at the State Democratic Convention in Sedalia endorsing the presidential candidacy of Grover Cleveland. Chiswell served as the secretary for the convention.

Chiswell was a fixture as delegate to both the state and national Democratic conventions and despite his not having held office for more than a decade, he had many callers attempting to convince him to launch candidacies for one office or another.

Though he was still enjoying his work at the *Democrat*, a return to politics was sorely tempting.

Despite that temptation, being a newspaper editor was a job Chiswell thoroughly loved.

Chiswell could look at the city he had called home for nearly a quarter of a century and see one of the most progressive small communities in Missouri.

Businesses were thriving, including Chiswell's newspaper and law office.

Chiswell invested money in modern equipment for the *Democrat*, operated by water power and what was described in a glowing profile of the city in the December 20, 1892 *Springfield News* as "the most complete and convenient printing machines of the present time."

As 1895 arrived and Chiswell, now 47 and continuing to be wooed for public office, took a pilgrimage in January with his wife of 23 years, Belle, to Maryland where he had spent his formative years.

The local newspaper, *The News of Fredericktown*, noted, "Lee Chiswell looks as if the west agreed with him and is as jolly as a school boy."

Chiswell looked forward to a long future with Belle and spoiling grandchildren once they arrived and he had many more productive years ahead of him at the newspaper and in politics.

Life was good for Lee Chiswell.

Until it all came crashing down.

In November 1895, Chiswell had his first bout of "the paralysis," or a stroke that kept him from being the person he had been.

Chiswell stepped down as editor of the *Democrat*, though he maintained ownership. A month later, the paralysis struck again.

It was the third attack that killed him on May 2, 1897, five months shy of his 50th birthday.

The newspaper that Lee Chiswell brought to prominence

wrote that his funeral was "probably the largest funeral ever held in Lamar" with more than 60 vehicles in the procession.

Businesses on the square closed as Chiswell's funeral was held in the Methodist Church.

One thing nearly everyone agreed on, the *Lamar Democrat* would never be the same.

Chiswell's obituary said as much.

"There is no one in this community that can fill his place."

With Chiswell's death, the *Democrat* fell upon hard times and went through multiple owners between Chiswell's death and the turn of the century.

Contrary to the opinion of most of those who lived in Lamar in the 1890s, the glory days of the *Lamar Democrat* not only were not over, they had yet to arrive.

CHAPTER FIVE

In the years following Lee Chiswell's death, the *Lamar Democrat* was a mere shell of what it had been during the nearly 13 years he had been at its helm.

Though Chiswell had left the business end of running the newspaper to his partners, it was he who steered the newspaper into its status as the dominant publication in Lamar as a powerful force in Democratic politics.

For the next few years, though new editions of the newspaper continued to be published every Thursday, the spice and flavor Chiswell brought to the *Democrat* were gone and were sorely missed.

At the same time the newspaper was mired in mediocrity, an unlikely young savior had started on the path that would eventually lead him to Lamar.

As it did with Chiswell, it was a westward migration that brought Arthur Fabian Aull to Barton County.

Aull was born November 18, 1872 in Kentucky. At the age of three, he lost his mother when she died in childbirth.

William Aull remarried in 1883 and a year later, he, his new wife and 12-year-old son moved to the Nashville Township in Barton County where he bought a farm.

Arthur Aull worked on the family farm and served as a hired hand on neighboring farms. He had developed a love of reading and spent the money he made from his various jobs on books.

After receiving his early education at the Nashville School, Aull pursued higher education at the Fort Scott, Kansas, Normal College, attending for two years hoping to become a lawyer.

Aull took a teaching position at his former school in Nashville, while studying law at night

Despite his busy schedule, Aull found the time to woo Luanna Turnbull, a Lamar girl.

They shared a love of reading and during the course of their courtship, she also become a teacher, taking a position at Nashville at the same time Aull was moving on to a higher-paying post as superintendent of the Mindenmines School District in western Barton County.

Arthur Fabian Aull and Luanna Belle Turnbull were married March 22, 1896 in Nashville.

In addition to his duties at the Mindenmines school, Aull tried his hand at Barton County politics and was elected county surveyor.

Then another opportunity presented itself and interested Aull greatly. One evening in 1899 he came home with news for Luanna, who remembers him being "quite excited."

"He heard that the *Lamar Democrat* was for sale again," Luanna recalled in an article she wrote for the newspaper in 1957.

The newspaper had changed hands several times since Chiswell's death, but was beginning to lose money for its latest

Arthur Aull. *Photo courtesy of Barton County Historical Society*

owners.

Teaching was a rewarding and fulfilling job, but it paid little, rarely exceeding more than $50 a month. Though publishing a newspaper had not been on his radar, with his love of reading and his keen interest in politics, it was a chance for Aull to achieve his ambitions.

Luanna was skeptical of the idea, but changed her mind after Aull convinced a Lamar banker to loan him the $6,000 he needed to become the new *Democrat* owner and in August 1900, Arthur Aull became the owner, publisher and editor of the *Lamar Democrat*.

CHAPTER SIX

Lamar's first marshal Wyatt Earp never returned to the city after his sudden departure in 1871, but his family maintained a presence in the community and in 1920, Walter and Emma Earp decided to move from their home outside of the city into Lamar.

Though the house had no special significance to them, they elected to buy the two-story white frame house on Kentucky Avenue where Martha Truman had given birth to a son 36 years earlier.

In a 1991 column in the *Lamar Democrat* and later in her book *Down Memory Lane*, Reba Earp Young recalled spending time at her grandparents' home.

"We four girls stayed with them a lot and helped with the work. We washed many tubs of clothes on the board and did big baskets of ironing and also we scrubbed the floor- the very floor the Trumans had walked on."

Of course, it was much later before that meant anything to Young.

"I'm sure there was a fence around the backyard," Young wrote, "and I think I remember there being a cow. Most townspeople did keep a cow back then for the family milk supply."

Young, who was in her 20s at the time, did not spend as much time with her grandparents as she would have liked because she was working as a teacher.

"My grandmother passed away on February 15, 1923, in the very room where Harry Truman first saw the light of day."

Harry Truman was serving his first and only term as Jackson County Court Eastern District judge when he returned to the town where he was born for the first time since his parents moved to Harrisonville in 1885.

Truman had not planned to come to Lamar. The visit was necessitated during a trip to Joplin to attend a convention at the Connor Hotel.

When he was about 40 miles from Joplin, Truman hit a pothole and damaged his car. He took a detour and had the repairs done at a shop in Lamar.

When Truman finally arrived in Joplin, he penned a letter that evening to his wife of five years, Bess, from the Connor Hotel.

In the letter, Truman devoted more words to the pothole that damaged his car and to the convention than he did to his first visit to his hometown.

His references to Lamar were limited to two sentences.

We had to make a detour and I went through Lamar, the first time I've been there since I was a year old. I couldn't see much change in the town except that Pop's old livery stable apparently is a garage now.

Truman's reference to not seeing much change likely came

from comparing what he saw to what his parents had told him about Lamar.

It would be another 10 years before Harry Truman returned, when he made his first visit as a candidate for U. S. Senate.

OO

By the time Harry Truman returned to the city of his birth, Arthur Aull had been at the helm of the *Lamar Democrat* for 34 years.

Even more than his predecessor Lee Chiswell, Aull had a passion for words and he was a far more gifted newsman than Chiswell.

Where Chiswell was a storyteller and limited his reporting, such as it was, to local, state and national politics, Aull had a curiosity about everything. He wrote about politics, but he also wrote about agriculture, business, social events, crime and anything else he thought would interest his readers. He especially had an affinity for the sensational.

In his biography of Aull, *All the News is Fit to Print*, Chad Stebbins reported that Aull's daily rounds began with a shave at one of the local barbershops and included "city hall, schools, the churches, the jails, the hospitals, the funeral homes and businesses around the square."

Perhaps the most important stop each day was the Barton County Courthouse where Aull not only gathered information from officeholders, but also picked up detailed descriptions of anything interesting that took place in criminal or civil court.

Aull wrote nearly every word in the newspaper, unlike many of the newspapers of that time, which relied on second-hand

Arthur Aull took daily walks with his dog Tippy around the Lamar square during the 1940s. *Photo courtesy of Barton County Historical Society*

stories from other newspapers to fill their pages.

The *Daily Democrat*, its publication frequency had been increased under Aull in 1904, had so much local news that some in the community could not believe that one man was responsible for all of it, something that still irritated Luanna Aull after her husband's death.

"Some of the 'wise ones' said, 'That young sprout isn't doing the writing. Tom Martin is doing it.' " Martin had been Aull's teacher and mentor and was about nine years older than Aull. But even the doubters soon realized that the voice that spoke to them from the pages of the *Lamar Democrat* was indeed the voice of Arthur Aull.

In Aull's world, everything that happened in the community was a news story. He wrote detailed descriptions of bitter divorces obtained from the court hearings, regaling readers with tales of infidelity, children born out of wedlock and drunken beatings.

In one such detailed divorce story, Aull wrote the following:

Frank Kester, a man in his early forties, was divorced from his wife, Verna Marie Kester. They were married in Colorado August 25th, 1915 and lived together about 18 months. She had an awful temper, he said, and would fly into a rage upon the most trivial occasion. She told him she didn't love him. She wouldn't cook his meals, not keep the house in order. She took night rides with other men and let them take indecent liberties with her. When he protested, she told him she would do as she pleased and for him to go to hell.

Such lurid detail, invariably told from the point of view of the spouse who was filing for divorce, often drew complaints and angry letters to the editor, all of which Aull ran word-for-word in the *Democrat*.

In the years before the advent of television and decades before the internet arrived, Arthur Aull's *Lamar Democrat* served not only as a source of news and information, but also provided daily entertainment for its ever-growing readership.

∞

After serving only one two-year term as the Jackson County Court's Eastern District judge, Harry Truman was defeated for re-election, one of many Democratic candidates swept away in the 1924 nationwide Republican wave that put Calvin Coolidge into the White House, but with the help of Kansas City's powerful Pendergast political machine he ran for Presiding Judge two years later and was elected.

During his two four-year terms, Truman steered building projects that changed the face of Jackson County, building roads, bridges and other public works projects that enhanced his reputation as a hard-working politician who could get things done.

Truman had thoughts of trying for statewide office, but did not receive machine boss Tom Pendergast's support. Reluctantly, after Pendergast's other choices turned him down, Truman received his backing for a U. S. Senate candidacy in 1934.

Arthur Aull, aware of Truman's connection to Lamar, wrote of his candidacy and his first campaign stop in the city in the May 25, 1934 *Democrat*, published 17 days after Truman's 50th birthday.

Despite Aull's preference for the Democratic Party and the name of his newspaper, his newspaper, unlike what it had been under the stewardship of his predecessors, did not serve as a propaganda outlet for the political party.

Aull's goal was to reach as many readers as possible and that could not be done if he immediately wrote off any customer who preferred the Republican Party.

Though his stories of crime and court news were often lurid, Aull offered more objective accounts of political stories, including the candidacy of the Independence politician who had been born in Lamar 50 years earlier.

The *Democrat* headlined its articles in bold capital letters, the same size as the remainder of the text of the article, followed by a description of what was in the article written in bold.

Often the entire article was covered in that description.

Aull's first article on Truman's candidacy was headlined "JUDGE TRUMAN CANDIDATE FOR U. S. SENATE STOPS OFF AT LAMAR WHICH WAS HIS BIRTHPLACE."

In the description below the main headline, Aull referred to Truman as an "eminent Kansas City contender for the U. S. Senate seat" and noted that the candidate was "the son of the late John Truman who was in the horse and mule business in Lamar from 1881 to 1885."

Aull's article did not indicate whether he had spoken with the candidate, but he offered this observation:

He is a man that as the ordinary folks come to know him they will like and respect. He likes to meet people, he has a level head and a straightforward way of putting things.

In the June 13, 1934 *Democrat*, Aull addressed the biggest negative Truman had been saddled with during his campaign-his connection with Tom Pendergast's powerful political machine and the concept being pushed by his opponent that Truman was a creation of Pendergast and was completely under his thumb.

As was his usual style in writing about politics, Aull did not betray any sign of favoring a candidate in the Democratic primary, even though one of the candidates was born in Lamar.

He noted that both Truman and his opponent, Congress-

Arthur Aull at his desk in the 1940s. *Photo courtesy of Barton County Historical Society*

man Jacob L. Milligan, were World War I veterans, then Aull addressed Truman's Pendergast connection.

Truman will be assailed because the Pendergast machine will support him. The idea seems to be in the state first to get this support if you can, then if you can't get it, cuss it and tell how awful it is.

Truman would use his own head in the Senate. Pendergast wouldn't even try to contact him.

The time would come when Aull's words about Truman would be nowhere near so kind.

As Truman competed in the race for the Democratic nomination, he returned to Lamar two months later and this time, the article in the July 31, 1934 *Democrat* offered more about him as a candidate, but not much more.

Judge Harry Truman of Independence spoke from the bandstand in the courthouse yard Friday forenoon at 10 o'clock. After his speech, which was short and very much to the point, he went about the square meeting as many folks as possible during his brief time in Lamar.

During Truman's speech, Aull wrote, the candidate attempted to appeal to Barton County farmers by telling of his own background in agriculture, managing the 640-acre Truman farm and said he could relate to the farmers' problems, including drought, flooding, low prices and mortgages.

Truman won the primary and then defeated his Republican opponent in November, buoyed by support from farmers, the American Legion and Jackson County.

In January 1935, the man who was born in Lamar stepped onto the national stage for the first time.

CHAPTER SEVEN

Truman's hold on his U. S. Senate seat was tenuous when it came time for re-election in 1940.

Though he was not Tom Pendergast's first choice to run for the Democratic nomination in 1934, there was no doubt that he was helped into the office by the Pendergast machine.

As 1940 arrived, the Pendergast machine had been crippled and Pendergast himself was sitting in a federal penitentiary after being convicted of not paying taxes.

The political boss's downfall came after Gov. Lloyd Stark, who Pendergast supported in 1936, turned on Pendergast. With the governor against him and Jackson County Prosecuting Attorney Maurice M. Milligan launching a campaign to clean up corruption, Pendergast's empire began crumbling.

With Pendergast no longer the major player in Missouri politics, it was expected that Harry Truman, who was sometimes derisively referred to as the Senator from Pendergast, would be swept away.

Stark, with an eye on making a name for himself on the national stage, took two steps in that direction. He filed to oppose Truman in the Senate primary and attended the 1940

Democratic National Convention in Chicago.

Stark hoped to burnish his growing reputation as the crusading governor who cleaned up Missouri and destroyed the corrupt Pendergast machine by making himself available for the vice presidential nomination.

While Roosevelt eventually selected Secretary of Agriculture Henry Wallace from Iowa to replace John Nance Garner to take the number two spot on the ticket, Stark still looked like a lock for election to the U. S. Senate.

The biggest obstacle for Stark was the third candidate in the primary- the other crusader who had just made his reputation bringing the Pendergast machine to its knees.

Stark's supporters were confident he could defeat the damaged Truman in a two-man race, but Milligan complicated the equation.

If Stark and Milligan split the anti-Truman vote, the man from Lamar just might be elected to a second term.

That was something the most powerful man in the city where Truman was born did not want to see happen.

Lamar Democrat publisher Arthur Aull devoured everything he could read about the corruption that Pendergast brought to the state of Missouri.

Though none of it had been linked to Truman, he was still Tom Pendergast's boy.

In his writing about the 1940 Democratic Senate primary, Aull abandoned the even-handed approach he employed six years earlier and turned the power of his newspaper against Harry Truman.

∞

During the last two weeks of the primary campaign, Arthur Aull made it clear whom he wanted to win the U. S. Senate seat and it was not the man who was born in the little house on Kentucky Avenue.

Though the *Democrat* was published daily with twice-weekly editions sent to those outside the normal readership area, few copies of the daily edition from the Aull era have been preserved.

In the twice-weekly edition, Aull included nearly all of his most important stories and as the primary race came to its conclusion, page one was filled with support for Gov. Lloyd Stark.

In the Friday, July 19, 1940 *Democrat*, Aull warned that the Pendergast machine was not dead yet, with the implication being that the only way you could get rid of it was to elect Stark and send Truman packing.

The remnants of the Pendergast machine feared Stark, Aull wrote and he even took issue with those who claimed Stark had accepted Pendergast's support in his gubernatorial bid, then betrayed him.

Stark was so far in the lead when Pendergast announced his support that it was merely a case for coming out for a winner.

After Stark was governor, Aull wrote, he discovered the extent of Pendergast's corruption and set out to dismantle the machine.

Truman made one stop in Lamar, speaking in front of the bandstand on the Barton County Courthouse lawn the morning of Monday, July 29.

Aull reported on the speech in the pages of that day's *Democrat*, describing the speech as "excellent," but the coverage, though not mentioning either of Truman's opponents, was weighted against the Lamar native from the opening paragraph in which he drew attention to the scandal that threated to make Truman a one-term senator.

We heard him make no reference to the Pendergast forces which have endorsed him and their opponents who are fighting him.

Instead, he confined his remarks to his own record in the Senate and as to what he and the other administration senators had done for the farmer and the common man.

Aull provided no details on what accomplishments Truman noted during his speech.

The *Democrat* editor, who was firmly behind Roosevelt's re-election, emphasized what Truman said about Roosevelt's Republican opponent, businessman Wendell Wilkie.

"He called attention to the fact that Wendell Wilkie was a utility magnate whose sympathies were all against what the Roosevelt Administration had sought to do for the people."

Aull concluded by writing, "In short, he made an excellent Democratic speech."

In addition to Aull's editorial decision to omit any of the accomplishments touted by Truman, he also left out one other fact that should have been considered pertinent information for his readers.

Unlike in Truman's first campaign six years earlier, Aull made no mention of the senator's being from Lamar.

In the next day's paper, Aull gave prominent page one play to the third candidate, Maurice Milligan, offering a detailed summary of Milligan's speech, which was also given from the bandstand on the Barton County Courthouse lawn.

Aull reported Milligan's shots at Stark, who Milligan said arrived late in the crusade against the Pendergast machine.

He included the prosecutor's attack on Truman.

He said Truman's nomination at the head of the Democratic ticket would smear the party with Pendergast from top to bottom and endanger the success of the whole ticket.

Aull saved his most potent salvos for the final few issues before the August 7 election.

On next Tuesday evening when the votes are counted, you will find that either Lloyd C. Stark or Harry S. Truman is the nominee for the Senate. The overwhelming majority of Democrats, because his victory would mark a great victory for the Pendergast machine, are against nominating Senator Truman.

Since they feel that way and there is no doubt that they do, even though they might prefer Honorable Maurice Milligan to Gov. Stark, they must admit that the facts which confront them prove their one way to leave no doubt about the defeat of Sen. Truman is to cast their ballots for Gov. Stark.

Aull by concluded by writing, "Let us all unite in this fight to give the old machine the knockout blow."

The power that Arthur Aull held in the City of Lamar and Barton County was never more in display than on August 7.

As Truman won resounding victories in neighboring Jasper and Newton counties, Stark overwhelmed him in Barton County, garnering 1,386 votes to 514 for Truman and 315 for Milligan.

Aull was right about the majority of Missouri Democrats wanting a change in their candidate for Senate. Stark and Milligan combined for more votes than Truman, but it was Truman who emerged from the primary, winning by a scant 8,000 votes.

In November, though once again hammered by Republican Manvel H. Davis about his connections to Pendergast,

Truman, who had easily won the general election six years earlier, received 51 percent of the vote to 49 percent for Davis, earning a second term and a steppingstone to a future that no one could have ever predicted.

CHAPTER EIGHT

Even with the patriotic fervor that was gripping Lamar and the United States in February 1941, no one held parades to honor the second man drafted into military service.

Only a day earlier Richard Freeman Chancellor, the 24-year-old son of Travelers Hotel owner H. C. Chancellor and his wife Pearl, watched as the first draftee was saluted by the community, complete with a gathering on the square and music from the Lamar High School Band.

Things did not work out as planned for the number one draftee, who flunked his physical when he reached Fort Leavenworth.

So draftee number two was summoned and had to get there by the next day.

Instead of crowds and stirring music sending him on his way, Richard Chancellor waited with his mother as the clock neared 3 a.m. for the bus to arrive at the Travelers Hotel.

Chancellor boarded the bus at 2:58 a.m., a time that re-mained forever etched in his mind.

When he arrived at Leavenworth, one of the first people he encountered was Captain B. L. Roberts, the former Lamar

High School principal and coach.

After he passed his physical and made it through basic training, Chancellor, despite his dream of flying, was placed in an armored unit at Fort Knox in Kentucky that had a mix of old timers and the new draftees.

The old timers did not like having us in their outfit. At all formations we were required to line up separately from the regulars and instead of bunking in the nice brick barracks, we were out on the porches, which were used for calisthenics, drill and instruction during inclement weather.

That location caused problems for Chancellor and the other draftees.

Being on the outside, it was impossible to keep the dust off our beds and equipment and as a result, we rarely passed inspection.

It was not long before Chancellor and some of the others who had college backgrounds gained the respect of the regulars with their technical expertise.

Chancellor was promoted to corporal and was assigned to accompany the battery commander at all times.

Chancellor and the First Armored Unit were sent along with other units to conduct field maneuvers during the first part of July 1941, first in Louisiana, then southern Arkansas and finally in the Carolinas.

The men in the unit knew the score.

"It was quite evident," Chancellor wrote years later, "that the government was of the belief that we would soon become involved in the war in Europe and they were preparing us as fast as they could with the equipment that was available which at that time was very outdated and scarce."

After months of maneuvers, the unit returned to Fort Knox December 7, 1941 and began unloading their trucks and taking their personal gear into the barracks.

"Pearl Harbor has been bombed by the Japanese," someone called out. During the rest of that day, as the men continued to unload the trucks, they listened to news accounts of what President Franklin D. Roosevelt described as "a day that would live in infamy."

It was a shock to all of us and especially to those of us who were draftees as we were nearing the end of our mandatory year of service and were looking forward to getting out.

As we learned, we had a lot more time to serve, but now we knew why.

After Pearl Harbor, Chancellor recalled, all leaves were canceled and training intensified.

"We were moved out of the barracks and into tents and new equipment started arriving and security was tightened."

Shortly after that, a notice was placed on the bulletin board that had a profound impact on Chancellor's life.

"The Army Air Corps would be coming through conducting interviews and testing for those who wanted to become members of combat crews."

Richard Chancellor would finally get his chance to fly.

By the beginning of 1942, the United States was at war with the Axis powers and Arthur Aull was standing firmly behind President Roosevelt and confident America would win the war.

Aull had predicted the coming of a second world war as early as 1935 and the entry of the U. S. into that war a full year before the Pearl Harbor bombing.

In a speech to the Joplin Rotary Club January 9, 1942, Aull outlined a vision of the post-war world that proved prophetic.

After the United States and her allies win the war, they must continue to use military might to maintain a better peace.

I rather hope the nation will become rather imperialistic and obtain and maintain important island bases in both the Atlantic and Pacific oceans. It has become necessary in the course of preserving future peace that I would nearly favor using our Army and Navy to police the world.

Arthur Aull. *Photo courtesy of Barton Count Historical Society*

Though Aull had not been successful in preventing Truman from winning the Democratic nomination for the Senate in 1940, the editor, who was entering his 43rd year at the *Democrat* was at the height of his influence and had built a national following.

During the '30s, Aull's small town newspaper had drawn

the attention of the national media, beginning with its prominent play in the syndicated humorous columns of Ted Cook, who worked at the *Los Angeles Examiner.*

Aull's graphic descriptions of the events in Lamar, which attracted both admirers and enemies locally, were often used as fodder for Cook's columns.

Though many had a hard time believing that Lamar existed or that the outlandish stories Aull told really happened, the *Democrat* began to develop a much greater circulation than newspapers in communities of 3,000 residents normally had.

The *Democrat's* subscription list included people from all over the United States since Hearst syndicated the Cook columns. Among the subscribers was movie star and comedian W. C. Fields.

Aull's fame increased even more as Truman became prominent on the national stage.

As the U. S. entered the Second World War, Aull was 69. Though he still approached his work with the same curiosity and boundless enthusiasm that kept nearly every one in Barton County reading the *Democrat* every day, five days a week, his health was beginning to deteriorate.

Aull's fame and influence were continuing to grow, but would he be around to enjoy the fruits of his labors?

CHAPTER NINE

After Richard Chancellor was accepted into the cadet program after the bombing of Pearl Harbor, he was given a leave while facilities were prepared for the fledgling airmen.

During his time off, he visited his nephew Don Davis, a music teacher in Marceline, Missouri.

Ione Williams was one of Davis' favorite Marceline High School students. In Davis' music appreciation class, she developed a fondness for classical music.

It surprised her when Davis extended an invitation to her.

"One day he said, 'Why don't you come by the apartment?' He and his wife lived in one of the nice apartments in Marceline. They were over the picture show, the Uptown. He wanted me to meet his wife and they took a liking to me."

When Davis confirmed when his nephew would arrive in Marceline, he told Ione Williams, "I'm just going to introduce you to him and I hope he likes you because you would make a good wife for him."

She was stunned.

"There I was only 15 years old and I hadn't had any thoughts of getting married or being anybody's wife."

Despite her reservations, Ione accepted the invitation and when they were introduced, she was immediately taken with Chancellor.

"He was a nice looking fellow. In fact, he was a handsome fellow and I thought, 'Why hasn't he got himself a wife,' if he was that interested, as nice looking as he was."

Ione soon found herself attracted to more than Chancellor's looks.

"He was a good conversationalist."

She learned of the time he had spent attending college and his deep interest in flying.

By the time their first meeting was over, Ione was quite taken with Richard Chancellor and the feeling was mutual.

"I was quite impressed with her," Chancellor wrote.

"It was the beginning of a beautiful and lasting romance."

It is impossible to understate the influence Arthur Aull had on the City of Lamar.

While the *Lamar Democrat* was justly known for its appeal to prurient interests, Aull also used the newspaper as a force for civic improvement. He was instrumental in the creation of the Lamar Chamber of Commerce, provided editorial support for public works projects and provided the backbone that help the community withstand efforts to organize a Ku Klux Klan chapter in the 1920s.

Even with his devotion to his newspaper and to the city of Lamar, Aull was that rarity-a driven man who never neglected his family life for his work.

"Arthur had a very happy faculty of leaving his business

cares behind him when he came home," Luanna Aull wrote. "He hurried in at evening with a merry greeting which was a signal for the family to gather around with the children eager to tell him the happenings of the day."

Often, Aull would not even reach the house before his daughters Madeleine, Genevieve and Betty greeted him outside and began the process of filling their father in on the day's events.

When Aull left the *Democrat*, the news of Lamar and Barton County was forgotten with his only interest the news that his wife and daughters shared.

"I never got to tell him any news after Madeleine learned to talk," Luanna said.

Madeleine Aull VanHafften adored her father. He had always been there for her, her mother and her sisters.

As Aull's health worsened, Madeleine, 46, returned to Lamar to be there for her father.

While Betty and Genevieve were inspired by their father to attend the University of Missouri School of Journalism, Madeleine did not, though that was her original plan.

"When I went away to Missouri University and told him I was going to major in journalism, he blew his top. He said, 'You'll do nothing of the sort! You'll take arts and sciences and learn things you need to know.' "

Aull, realizing his twilight years had arrived, needed Madeleine's help to keep the *Democrat* running efficiently, but her presence also solved another problem for the *Democrat* editor.

"My father told me I was the one who should take over the newspaper because he wouldn't have to pound journalism schooling out of my head like he would have had to do with my sisters," Madeleine recalled.

With Madeleine's return to Lamar, Aull had not only had help at his newspaper, but he had charted a course for its future.

Harry Truman entered his second term in the Senate battered and bruised from the attacks he received from Republicans and from his Democratic opponents in his re-election campaign.

It did not take long for Truman to put his Pendergast connection in the past, occasionally to be brought up but never with the same success it nearly had in 1940.

On February 10, 1941, only a month after the beginning of his second term, Truman, convinced that the military's massive $10 billion plus buildup in preparation for possible entry into the European war was riddled with waste, inefficiency and corruption, asked the Senate for permission to form a special committee.

Harkening back on his years dealing with governmental contracts as a Jackson County judge, Truman told his colleagues, "I have never yet found a contractor, who if not watched, would not leave the government holding the bag."

Truman received the go-ahead, but there was concern in the Roosevelt administration that Truman's special committee might be used by some of its members, perhaps Truman himself, as an excuse for grandstanding and making names for themselves by embarrassing the Administration.

When Truman asked for the modest sum of $25,000 to fund the committee, he received only $15,000, but he made that amount work and soon impressed the Senate and the Administration with his diligence, his selection of skilled investigators rather than political hacks and, most of all, by the results the Truman Committee achieved.

Though it continued to have its critics, primarily those who had been benefiting from the corruption and waste, the committee and its chairman earned a reputation for thorough investigations, sound suggestions for improvements and its completely bipartisan nature.

The committee's decisions were all unanimous, something unthinkable in the 21st Century and unusual in 1941.

The Truman Committee's investigations also forced the military to face harsh truths about outdated equipment and areas in which the buildup was not functioning as rapidly as it should.

After the bombing of Pearl Harbor, the committee's work became even more important and with that importance its chairman found himself in the national spotlight receiving praise for his efforts to make sure the United States military was at its best as the lives of thousands of young men were at risk.

In a short time, the senator from Missouri had gone from being considered the corrupt puppet of a political machine to being talked about as a possibility for higher office.

And with FDR's penchant for changing his vice presidents, that could happen as soon as 1944.

Truman was not the only one with a Lamar connection making national news, though Arthur Aull probably would have preferred it if he had not been.

On August 12, 1943, Associated Press, relying on Aull's

colorful account, printed the story of his violent encounter with two women.

Arthur Aull, veteran publisher of the Lamar Democrat, was nursing a cut and a bruised head today, the result of an encounter with two irate women readers, one of whom wielded a club.

As might be expected, the beating came as a result of one of Aull's daily excursions into detailed accounts of domestic squabbles.

The woman struck Aull on the head eight to 10 times. Aull took a taxi home and a doctor was summoned to treat the wounds. Aull, though still bleeding, recognized a good story and while he waited for the doctor to arrive, he dictated the sordid tale of his beating to daughter Madeleine.

Despite the pain, Aull lost none of his characteristic wit and concluded the dictation on an optimistic note.

Fortunately, we wore our old straw hat, which was some protection, and we have a rather heavy head of hair which protected us some. It would certainly have ruined a bald headed guy with no hat.

CHAPTER TEN

Richard Chancellor reported to Kelly Field in San Antonio, Texas as a member of Class 43B.

It was 1942 and the nation was at war.

"For the next six weeks, the only plane we saw was from textbooks."

It was out of bed before dawn, marching and calisthenics, followed by a full day of studying navigation, Morse Code and military laws and customs.

Chancellor and the others in Class 43B received no breaks. The schedule continued day after day, seven days a week for the full six weeks.

Each night, he took pen to paper and wrote Ione and on those evenings when he received return letters, he read and reread them looking forward to the day when he would see her again.

Not all of the students made it through 43B.

"The physical part of the training was probably the hardest and accounted for a lot of washouts," Chancellor said.

After Kelly Field, the next stop for Chancellor and other cadets was Parks Air College in East St. Louis, Illinois.

At last, Chancellor was going to fly.

"Parks was a civilian school under contract to the Air Corps to get us started in the basics of flying with an emphasis on safety and on aerobatics."

Chancellor's instructor was a short man named Mr. Gil, "a little man with a hot temper," he recalled, but the man knew his subject and led the cadets through what Chancellor described as "a thrilling series of maneuvers which we would need."

Again, as at Kelly Field, there were many who did not make it through the training, some washed out due to lack of coordination and some of their volition.

"We were fortunate that our class had no fatalities."

∞

For the next year and a half, Chancellor distinguished himself, not only as a capable airman, but also as a top-notch pilot and leader of men.

Both abilities came into play during a bombing mission over southern Italy on September 15, 1943, when his plane experienced mechanical difficulties.

The mission had been a successful one, bombing the railroad junction in Potanza, and the planes were returning to the base and flying over the Mediterranean.

"Dick noticed a peculiar reaction of the ship to his control," Lt. Joe Young, bombardier, recalled. "He told Carter to take over. Parker and myself were up front in the nose.

"Dick called me up on the flight deck, told me the situation and said for me to go back to the rudder to see if I could fix it. I went back with the engineer."

It was obvious there was nothing that could be done. "The rudder and elevator were locked in a descent and right turn altitude."

After relaying the information to Chancellor, he told the crew what needed to be done. They would have to ride the plane to the ground and hope for the best.

"We threw everything overboard- guns, ammunition, parachutes and everything we could pick up. It took time to do this and all the time we were getting further out to sea."

Chancellor handed Young his knife, so the rafts could be cut when the plane crashed.

"It was the best flying I have ever seen," Young said. "When we hit, Dick and Carter went through the windshield. They were not cut up at all. Carter had a pin scratch on one hand."

Both men were shaken by the impact.

"I had the escape hatch open when we hit and fortunately, it stayed open," Young recalled. "As we hit, the top turret broke loose from the fuselage and came thundering down.

"I saw it cut the two boys inside, good boys- the assistant engineer and radio man- in two. The turret caught me in the chest and the armor plate that is behind the pilot's seat, which Carter was in, caught me in the waist. By the grace of God, I managed to tear out of this by going still deeper into the water as it had already filled the plane."

When Young climbed out, he saw Chancellor and another crew member on the right wing. They had inflated one raft. Young went to another compartment, retrieved a second raft and began inflating it.

Chancellor dived into the water to attempt to rescue the tail gunner and another crew member.

Young credited Chancellor's bravery for the rescue of the

two. The tail gunner had suffered a broken neck.

"Carter was paddling toward the ship, so I pulled him into the raft and by the time Dick had the boys about out of the ship and had inflated their Mae West life belts.

Chancellor, exhausted after his efforts, was clinging to the left wing when Young and other crew members pulled him into the raft.

When everyone had boarded, Chancellor took a count of who was there- eight men had been rescued.

Eleven had been on board when the mission began.

Chancellor never got over the loss of the other three.

CHAPTER ELEVEN

Two hours after Chancellor and his men were in the sea, they spotted a British plane, which swooped down just above them and then left and never reappeared.

Chancellor determined they would remain near the wreckage with the thought that it would be easier for planes to see them.

Night came and it was a restless one for the eight men.

After daybreak, they took inventory and it did not take long.

Their supplies included 60 ounces of water, one four-ounce can of pork meat, and some chocolate that had been contaminated by the salt water.

Bombardier Joe Young had one pack of soggy cigarettes.

The only equipment the men had was a compass and a fishing line.

As the second night arrived, they took their first drink of water.

Three times their hopes for a swift rescue were dashed as planes flew by. They shot flares, but the flares had not been spotted.

When it was daytime, the men put their underwear over their heads to protect them from the sun and began rowing the rafts.

An encounter with a school of porpoises nearly wrecked the vessels.

At one point, they thought they saw land, but that was not the case. Chancellor talked to his men, trying to boost their morale.

Not only were they stranded at sea, but the tail gunner with his broken neck was immobile, lying on his back the entire time.

"We paddled like hell, playing the currents and going northwest by the compass at day and the stars at night," Young recalled.

When they finally rested for a couple of hours, their break was interrupted.

Chancellor heard a noise and when he looked up, he saw two German U-boats.

"We laid quiet and floated with the currents until they were no longer in sight, then began rowing again," Young said.

Chancellor and the crew gave most of their water to the tail-gunner. Little remained.

Around noon the next day, they spotted two transport planes. Chancellor fired the flares, but there was no response.

Later that afternoon, they spotted two more planes. Chancellor waited until the planes were even with the rafts and fired a flare.

The planes swooped down, dropped a five-gallon tin of water and notes saying that one plane would stay with then while the other would make sure that a ship came to rescue them.

"We knew the angels were here," Young said.

"It was the happiest day of our lives."

CHAPTER TWELVE

In the years before the United States entered the war, the Lamar Square served as the favored destination for young people of high school age or a few years older.

On Friday and Saturday nights, especially during the summer months, but any time when the weather was halfway decent, groups of young people in cars began the process of cruising the square early in the evening and continued for hours.

The art of cruising is a particularly American one and not confined to Barton County, Missouri. Visitors from foreign countries fail to see the attraction of circling a small area, passing the same scenery and often the same people for hours.

Sometimes the young people would park their cars and talk to each other, but often the conversations were shouted over the sound of the running motors of their vehicles.

The endless driving was curtailed considerably during the years when gasoline was rationed to support the war effort, but in those years before the war and for decades afterward, though the models and makes of the cars and pickup trucks changed dramatically, the art of cruising remained remarkably the same.

The Lamar square was a place for young people to meet, let off steam from the drudgery of school, work, and family chores, meet with attractive people of the opposite sex, and more than occasionally for some, enjoy alcoholic beverages.

In the young people's minds, the Lamar Square was a secret place, far from the prying eyes of adults, who, of course, had no idea of what happened there.

Many of those same adults now understood the worries they put their parents through when they cruised the Lamar Square during their teen years.

The attraction of the square was not limited to Lamar youth.

It was perhaps even more appealing to teens and young adults from smaller, neighboring communities, many of whom looked on Lamar, a city of about 3,000 residents, as the big city and the square as a place of wonder.

Any Friday or Saturday night, it was easy to find young people from Golden City, 17 miles to the east, Liberal, 14 miles to the west, Jasper 12 miles south and even as far away as Lockwood 25 miles east.

And in the late '30s, there was always a contingent from Sheldon, 12 miles north of Lamar just past the Barton/Vernon County line.

One of those young people was a gregarious young man who treated each person he met as if that person was a good friend and was the most important person in the world at that moment.

It was not pretense on Gerald Gilkey's part. From the beginning, he had a genuine interest in people and enjoyed being around them.

Longtime Lamar mayor and car dealership owner Gerald Gilkey in 1938, seated in his first car, a 1924 Model T which he painted a bright yellow. *Photo courtesy of the Gilkey family*

People in Sheldon, Lamar and the surrounding communities knew who he was, but Gilkey's winning personality was not the only thing that made him stand out on the Lamar Square.

He was also the only person anyone knew who had a canary yellow 1924 Model T.

It was standard issue black when Gilkey bought it for either $17 or $19 from Gerald Beeny of Sheldon in 1938. It was his first car and the 16-year-old wanted it to stand out.

It did.

Local law enforcement also knew who Gilkey was, though mostly for the same reason everyone else did. He was a likable young man.

There were the occasions when the fun-loving Gilkey became quite a handful for local law enforcement, including the time he and his friends tied a tire to the back of his car, set it afire and drove around the square.

"Gerald Gilkey, go home," a policeman shouted.

Gilkey went home, but he kept coming back until eventually he decided never to leave.

An hour and a half after the planes spotted Richard Chancellor and his crew on their rafts in the Mediterranean, a British mine sweeper rescued the eight men, fed them and provided them with baths and clean clothes.

There would be many stops before they arrived, but finally, they were safe and headed home.

When he returned to the states in February 1944, a ceremony was held awarding Chancellor a medal for "bravery beyond the call of duty" for rescuing the two soldiers who had been trapped in the plane wreckage.

Soon after the award ceremony, Lt. Richard Chancellor was headed overseas.

The war was far from over.

For the owner of the Travelers Hotel in Lamar, Henry Columbus Chancellor, better known as H. C. and his wife Pearl, having the opportunity to see their son honored for his bravery was one of the proudest moments of their lives.

A few months earlier, the War Department notified them that Richard was missing in action and they feared the worst-

A post card of Travelers Hotel.

they would never see their son again.

Thankfully, the wait for the good news, though it seemed to take an eternity, was mercifully a short one.

The Chancellors came to Lamar in 1932 when H C. bought the Travelers Hotel and in the years since, he had turned it into the most successful hotel in the city.

Perhaps the biggest day in the long history of the hotel was only a few months away, though no one knew it at the time.

It was going to be busy time for H. C. Chancellor.

An even more eventful few months were in store for his son.

As much as Gerald Gilkey loved to come to Lamar to see the pretty girls who made the weekly pilgrimage to the square, it turned out he did not even have to leave Sheldon to find the girl who would win his heart.

Though he did not have to leave home to meet her, the road that led him to Sheldon High School student Betty Medlin took Gilkey far from Sheldon.

After he graduated from high school in 1939 at age 17, Gilkey attended college for one year at Kansas State Teachers College in Pittsburg, just across the Missouri/Kansas state line.

After one year, Gilkey and some friends decided to head west to seek their fortune.

For a time he picked hops, but with the meager amount he earned, it was obvious he was not going to make his fortune any time soon.

The next stop was Seattle where Gilkey worked in a grocery store for a few months.

Finally, he returned home and found himself attracted to a player on the Sheldon High School girls basketball team.

"He asked if he could take me home after a game," Betty Gilkey recalled.

Betty's parents, John and Lola Medlin, did not approve of this older man (Gilkey was 20 at the time) pursuing their daughter.

"He was persistent," Betty said. "If he made up his mind, that's the way it was going to be."

One time taking her home was going to be it, but Betty made sure it did not happen that way.

"I left my uniform in his car and he brought it back to me the next day."

After that, the two were inseparable, much to the disapproval of her parents.

Several months after they began seeing each other, they realized they wanted to spend their lives together and they decided to get married, but told no one.

"My parents did not know we were getting married," Betty said. "I was still in high school."

The wedding took place June 18, 1942, at the home of a minister friend in Webb City, Missouri, about 50 miles south of Sheldon.

"Gerald had carried the marriage license for two months," Betty said.

It took only two days for the newlyweds' secret to be revealed.

It was only a small item buried on page three of the June 20, 1942 *Joplin Globe*, the regional daily newspaper that served several southwest Missouri counties and communities, including Sheldon.

Headlined "Sheldon couple weds" and carrying a June 19 Webb City dateline, the news was broken to the Gilkey and Medlin families in this way:

Miss Betty Jo Medlin and Gerald W. Gilkey, both of Sheldon, Missouri were married at 7 o'clock last night by Rev. Alfred E. Jenkins, pastor of the Emmanuel Baptist Church. The ceremony was performed in Jenkins' home on North Ball Street.

Betty's family reacted in an unexpected fashion. "They decided 'we're going to get behind them and we're going to help them.'"

The Gilkeys were only able to enjoy being together for three months. In September 1942, Gerald Gilkey received his draft notice. He took his preliminary examination September 25 in Springfield, Missouri, then on September 29, he was sworn into the U. S. Army.

After their goodbyes, Betty Gilkey returned to Sheldon.

"It was three years before I saw him again."

CHAPTER THIRTEEN

Three years and eight months earlier, Harry S Truman had eked out a victory by the narrowest margin in his bid for re-election to the U. S. Senate.

Now in the jam-packed convention hall in Chicago, Truman was accepting the nomination to be the vice presidential candidate on the 1944 Democratic national ticket.

Truman lost the first ballot and was barely leading over the incumbent vice president Henry Wallace on the second when party leaders, wanting to keep Wallace from being put in a position where he would succeed Roosevelt if the president died, applied pressure and cut deals and when the ballot closed, the delegates approved Truman by a wide margin.

As Truman began his speech, Mattie Truman, 91, who had given birth to the vice presidential nominee 60 years earlier in that small house on Kentucky Avenue in Lamar, sat in a rocking chair in the one-story Missouri bungalow where she lived with her daughter Mary.

It was the same rocking chair she sat in as she listened with growing anger to the speeches during the Republican Convention, which had been held June 26-28, also in Chicago.

Bess, Harry and Margaret Truman at the 1944 Democratic National Convention in Chicago. *Photo courtesy of Truman Library and Museum*

"I tried not to hate them," she told a United Press reporter, adding that they kept saying things that brought her to the brink of hating them.

"They keep predicting that Roosevelt will die in office if he's elected. The Republicans hope he will. They keep saying I'll die, too, and I'm almost 92. I hope Roosevelt fools them."

During that interview, Mattie Truman, who had been a widow since 1914, confided she did not want her son to receive the vice presidential nomination.

"I want him to stay in the Senate where he can do more good."

The good he had been doing in the Senate is what propelled him into a position where he was the delegates' choice.

Truman entered his second term still trying to shed his "Senator from Pendergast" label and thanks to the Truman Committee and the key role it was playing in the war effort, Truman was no longer considered to be a faceless machine politician.

Truman began his speech by thanking the delegates for "this very great honor which has come to the great State of Missouri.

"There is also connected with it a great responsibility, which I am perfectly willing to assume."

He concluded, "I accept this honor with all the humility that a citizen of the United States can assume in this position."

Truman was only the fourth Missourian to be nominated for vice president and the first from a major party. None had ever run on a successful ticket.

In her interview with the UP reporter, Mattie Truman, though not wanting to see her son receive the nomination, said if he was the choice, she was ready to go to bat for his candidacy.

"I'm not too old to campaign yet," she said. "I don't care what people say about us old folks."

∞

The minute the Democratic Convention nominated Truman as its vice presidential candidate, Lamar community leaders, despite the city and Barton County's firm rejection of Truman in the 1940 Democratic primary, saw an opportunity to promote the city.

Almost immediately after the convention, while drinking coffee in the Travelers Hotel dining room with owner H. C.

Chancellor, Mayor Guy Ross and Lamar Chamber of Commerce President Raymond River, both Republicans, devised the idea of inviting Truman to return to Lamar and open his campaign.

Since Ross had met Truman once, though they were by no means friends, he was the one who wrote the message.

The following telegram was sent to Truman:

Hon. Harry S. Truman

Stevens Hotel

Chicago, Illinois

The people of Lamar, regardless of party, are proud of you and invite you to open your campaign in the city of your birth.

The telegram was signed by Guy Ross, mayor, Raymond River, president Chamber of Commerce, William S. Lowery, commander Jesse C. Rains Post 209 and R. F. Ryder, commander Yowell Frow Post 3691.

One of the biggest proponents of the Truman invitation was the man who had turned his newspaper's influence against Truman four years earlier. Arthur Aull's earlier negative feelings against Truman, largely a result of the information that was revealed about the Pendergast machine when it was dismantled, had changed as he read of the diligent work the senator and his committee were doing to aid the war effort by improving efficiency and rooting out corruption.

Aull was also firmly in favor of anything that he would help the city where he had lived for the past 44 years.

It is believed there will be a great outpouring to hear Sen. Truman if he did this and it would give Lamar more advertising.

Aull delivered his revised assessment of the man who had just replaced him as the best-known person from Lamar.

(Truman) is a realist and a man who believes things ought to

be run on the basis of what they are. He will give the campaign a
real honest-to-God shot in the arm.

Aull added that Truman was "a man of direct action who believes the campaign should be realistic and straight from the shoulder."

Despite the enthusiasm of Ross, River and Aull, the general consensus was that, while the invitation was worth a try, the chances were almost non-existent that Truman would open his campaign in a town the size of Lamar, a town he had left when he was 10 months old and visited on only a couple of occasions since then.

Since John and Mattie Truman left Lamar in 1885, their son had made a brief stop for a few hours in 1924, little noted by most Lamar residents, then stops during the 1934 and 1940 Senate campaigns.

His home was in Independence, so it took nerve for Ross and River to believe they could convince him to come to a city that had showed a marked preference for Lloyd Stark four years earlier.

On the other hand, if Truman rejected the proposal, all they were out was the time it took to compose the message and the cost of the telegram.

What did they have to lose?

On August 8, National Democratic Party Chairman Robert Hannegan announced Truman would "probably" come to Lamar on August 29 but President Roosevelt would make the final decision.

When a week passed and Lamar city officials had yet to hear from anyone, Mayor Ross sent a telegram to Hannegan asking if he had any more information.

Meanwhile, an executive committee consisting of Ross,

During this August 18, 1944 meeting at the White House, Franklin D. Roosevelt gave Truman his approval to accept the vice presidential nomination at Lamar. *Photo courtesy of Truman Library and Museum*

River, VFW Post Chairman Rubey Rider and American Legion Post Chairman William Lowery was named to organize the Truman appearance if it happened.

Finally, on Friday, August 18, Truman met with Roosevelt.

As was his habit when they were apart, Truman described the meeting in a letter to Bess, beginning by telling her,

Wish you'd been here for the White House luncheon today. Lunch was announced and we went out into the backyard of the White House under an oak tree planted by old Andy Jackson and the movie men and the flashlight boys went to work. He finally got hungry and ran 'em out.

Then his daughter, Mrs. Boettiger, acted as hostess and expressed a lot of regret that you were not there. I told the President that you were in Missouri attending to my business there and

he said that was O. K. He gave me a lot of hooey about what I could do to help the campaign and said he thought I ought to go home for an official notification and then go to Detroit for a labor speech and make no more engagements until we had had another conference.

So that's what I am going to do.

Truman concluded the letter writing, "Kiss Margie. Lots and lots of love to you," and signed it "Harry."

When Truman left his meeting with Roosevelt, he was carrying two red roses, one given to him by Roosevelt to present to his wife Bess, while the other came from Roosevelt's daughter to give to his daughter Margaret.

Truman told reporters he would open his campaign in Lamar on August 31 and then make a Labor Day speech in Detroit and that he hoped the Democratic National Committee would not ask him to make too many speeches, since his Senate committee had a considerable amount of work to do.

With Roosevelt already making it known he would not be campaigning (and his health certainly not permitting it, anyway), the Truman speech would not only be Truman's first major speech, but it would launch the Democratic presidential campaign.

That guaranteed the attention of the nation would be focused on Lamar, Missouri.

The event, no doubt, would attract thousands, as well as representatives of the national radio networks, the wire services and the major newspapers.

Nothing like this had ever happened in Lamar and there was real doubt whether the city could pull it off.

Still, the news of Truman's visit came at a time when the city desperately needed an entertaining distraction.

Recent events had cast an air of sadness over the city.

A visit from Harry Truman might be just the tonic the people of Lamar needed.

CHAPTER FOURTEEN

—— ○○ ——

Though *Lamar Democrat* readers still eagerly pored over Arthur Aull's fevered descriptions of drunk driving arrests, bar fights and divorce proceedings, the U S. was a nation at war and the locals hungrily devoured every bit of information Aull provided about the war effort and about the role the local boys were playing in it.

Nearly every Barton County family had someone who was serving his country, some overseas, some on U. S. bases. Aull printed every scrap of information he could find and his readers appreciated it.

Most of the time, the coverage was matter of fact, but when the community needed it, Aull knew what he needed to write and the words came from the heart.

Such was the case when the city of Lamar suffered its second casualty of the war August 12 on the battlefields of France.

In a page one story, Aull broke the news of Donald Quillin's death to his readers.

Don was as fine a looking soldier as one ever saw. He was a little over six feet tall, lithe, strong and bronzed. He looked the part of the finest America had to offer in her fighting men.

The word came in a message from the War Department to his parents, Mr. and Mrs. Charley Quillin Thursday evening.

The news ran like an electric shock all over town. Donald is the first Lamar boy to have given his life on the French field of battle. He will sleep until the end of war in one of the soldiers' cemeteries in France.

Donald was born near Newport on April 12, 1919. He attended the Lamar Schools and graduated from high school with the Class of 1938.

He was a popular and handsome son and had many friends in Lamar. He was the apple of his mother's eye and Lamar people heard the news with the greatest feeling of sorrow for his mother and her family.

The loss of this gallant and young Lamar boy has brought the war and its tragedy ever closer to Lamar.

Each day we receive news of war casualties for this county, but often they are preceded, sometimes for months, by the message "missing in action," and though the grief and uncertainty are harrowing, the final message of death does not come with such a shock to the families and friends of the boys.

Lamar has suffered two losses by death in the field of battle, Earl Overton and now Donald.

She has also lost two other boys, Roy Sumners and Wilson Travis for whom, though their deaths have never been officially confirmed, small hope is held.

Tragedy was no stranger to Henry Columbus Chancellor. It had been a constant companion for him his entire adult life.

His first wife died in childbirth, while the second fell victim to tuberculosis, leaving him with two-year-old daughter Ruby.

He found love yet a third time, marrying Pearl. The couple had four children- the eldest Harold, Marguerite, Richard and the fourth, a daughter Crystal, who died of whooping cough when she was nine months old.

H. C. Chancellor persevered in spite of the setbacks. After growing up in Barton County, he moved to Kansas where at one time he owned a newspaper. Moving back to Missouri, he served three terms in the state legislature and returned to Barton County in 1932 when he bought the Travelers Hotel, when his son Richard was 11.

H. C. Chancellor read the *Democrat* every day and it was not easy for him to read Arthur Aull's description of the death of Donald Quillin.

While he grieved for the sacrifice made by a soldier far too young to die who had given his life for his country, Chancellor, too, had received bad news from the War Department.

Less than a year earlier, his son Richard had been one of those who had been officially listed as "missing in action," but he had survived.

Once again, Richard Chancellor was missing in action.

Was Arthur Aull right?

Could the next message from the War Department be the one telling him his son was never going to return?

CHAPTER FIFTEEN

Hite's Phillips 66 truck stop in Jasper, Missouri, 12 miles to the south of Lamar, was one of the few places in that area of Missouri that remained open 24 hours a day.

Situated on busy Highway 71 at a time when a driver could take a trip across the highways of America and be able to see a city without taking an off-ramp, Hite's was a regular stop for those drivers, especially truckers, who needed gasoline, a sandwich, a piece of pie and a cup of coffee before returning to the road.

At 2:30 a.m. August 17, 1944, the only two people at Hite's were the night attendant, Pearce Hastings, and 16-year-old waitress Lilly Bemis.

Bemis, the second oldest of six children, used her pay and tips to help the family since her mother stayed at home and cared for her younger siblings and her father did his best with the pay he received as an over-the-road truck driver, but with a large family it always helped to have more.

The silence of the night was interrupted when three men, two of them standing about six feet tall and the other one a few inches shorter, appearing to be in their early to mid-20s, entered and ordered coffee.

When Lilly returned with the coffee, she found one of the men pointing a .32 caliber pistol in her direction, while another wielded a long-barreled weapon and trained it on Hastings.

The third man opened the cash register and removed between $130 and $140 and gas rationing stamps then forced Hastings to hand over his wallet, which contained $29.59.

The man with the rifle took Hastings out to their black Ford and had him fill up the tank, about eight dollars worth.

Moments later, the three men peeled out of Hite's and headed north on Highway 71.

As soon as he could get back into the building, Hastings phoned Barton County Sheriff Roy Patterson at his home. Patterson's wife Hazel answered.

Her husband was exhausted after driving to Springfield on county business the previous day and she hoped this might not be something he would need to handle.

When she heard Hastings' excited tone, she called her husband to the phone and listened in on the extension as Hastings told Patterson what happened, described the men and the car and let him know the three men were headed in his direction.

Patterson went to his son Sammie's room and asked if he would drive and told him to "get the guns.

Sammie had not planned to still be in Lamar. Immediately after his graduation from Lamar High School three months earlier, he attempted to enlist in the Army, but flunked his physical due to a hand injury.

Hazel Patterson shouted at them to "be careful" as they jumped into Patterson's car.

It was the last time she saw them alive.

OO

Ira Farmer, who raised cattle on land about a mile west of Lamar, was awakened at approximately 4 a.m. by a series of loud noises that he thought sounded like a car backfiring.

When Farmer looked outside to investigate, he saw two parked cars and a few moments later, he saw one of the cars heading east at a high rate of speed.

Rather than wait to see what the driver of the other car would do, Farmer returned to bed.

At daybreak, after eating breakfast, he tended his cattle and saw the other car was still there with the passenger side door open and a man's legs hanging out.

Figuring the man was sleeping, Farmer continued his chores, but when he finished, the car was still there and the man's legs were still hanging out, appearing to be in the exact same position they were in earlier.

Fearing what he was going to find, Farmer approached the car and was greeted by an image that he would never forget.

Inside the car were the blood-soaked bodies of Barton County Sheriff Roy Patterson and his son, Sammie.

Roy Patterson's feet were on the ground, but the upper portion of his body was slumped over on the seat. Sammie Patterson's head was slumped over the steering wheel, with his foot on the brake.

Farmer returned to his house and called Raymond River, who not only was Lamar Chamber of Commerce president, but also was the owner of River Funeral Home and served as Barton County coroner.

River contacted Patterson's chief deputy Joshua Box and

Barton County Sheriff Roy Patterson.
Photo courtesy of Barton County Historical Society

within 10 minutes, River and deputies were on the scene.

Roy Patterson's gun was empty, while their other weapon, a shotgun, had not been fired.

The killer shot the sheriff three times, with one of the bullets hitting him in the back of the neck and exiting just below his eye. He had also been shot in the right ear.

Sammie Patterson, who was unarmed when he was killed, was shot just once, with the fatal bullet hitting him just below the left ear.

As River examined the bodies, Box contacted the Highway Patrol and a photographer was sent from Springfield to take pictures of the crime scene.

Within an hour, word of the Pattersons' fate was spreading in Lamar.

One of the first to hear about it was *Democrat* Publisher Arthur Aull.

He, like many of those who had lived in Lamar for years, could not believe that something like this could happen again.

The murders of another Barton County Sheriff, John Harlow, and his 18-year-old son Dick at the Barton County Jail in 1919 had stunned the city and led to a crime that was just as horrific- and marked the only time in the 44 years he had been editor and publisher of the *Lamar Democrat* that Aull hid the truth from his readers.

More than 25 years before the murders of Roy and Sammie Patterson, Barton County learned that another sheriff and his 18-year-old son had been brutally murdered during an escape from the county jail.

Jay Lynch, a career criminal with a lengthy record was hiding out at his sister's place in the Verdella area of Barton County when law enforcement became aware Lynch was sought by federal authorities for robbing boxcars.

After Lynch was arrested, Sheriff John Harlow arranged to take him back to St. Louis where his federal crimes had been committed.

As the sheriff was preparing to leave the Barton County Jail to catch the train, Lynch asked if he could make a phone call to his wife, who was staying with his sister.

Patterson agreed.

What happened next was detailed by Arthur Aull in the March 6, 1919 *Democrat*.

As Lynch ceased to talk, he suddenly whipped a revolver from his clothes, no one knows just where, pointed it at the sheriff and told him to put up his hands.

Then Lynch opened fire. One bullet struck the sheriff in the left breast, a short distance above the nipple, was deflected by a rib, went out the left side of his chest and grazed the arm.

Another bullet entered the chest up almost the same distance above the nipple, about an inch and a quarter from the other, ranged to the right, went through the breast bone and came out under the right arm.

The sheriff's family was at the jail, his wife only a short distance from Harlow when he died. Lynch then shot Harlow's son, leaving him mortally wounded. Dick Harlow managed to cling to life for a few days, but took a turn for the worse causing Mrs. Harlow to have to leave her husband's funeral to be with their son.

Hounds were brought in from Carthage and Springfield to help search for Lynch, but he managed to escape and was captured a few days later in LaJunta, Colorado.

Justice, at least the kind that takes place in a courtroom, happened quickly as Lynch pleaded guilty to the murders on May 18, 1919, in Barton County Circuit Court.

Since the state of Missouri had outlawed the death penalty in 1917, Judge B. G. Thurman sentenced Lynch to life in prison.

The sentence was never carried out.

Lynch and his family were taken into Judge Thurman's chambers to protect him until he could be transported out of town.

The killer talked with his wife and was allowed to hold the baby. He had just handed the baby back to her when the mob broke through the door and overpowered the guards.

"My God, boys. You aren't going to hang me, are you?" Lynch said. It was a far cry from earlier in the courtroom when he said he would prefer a hanging to spending life in the penitentiary.

As the two dozen men who had burst through the door dragged Lynch out, placing a rope around his neck, Lynch's wife shouted, "My God," and fainted, dropping the baby, which thankfully was caught before it hit the hardwood floor.

The mob dragged Lynch over furniture, through the hallway, out the door and then down the courthouse steps, his skull bouncing off each as the procession continued.

A crowd of more than 500 gathered on the north side of the Barton County Courthouse and cheers erupted as they saw Jay Lynch and the rope around his neck.

John Harlow's widow watched from a car parked on the side of the square.

The first attempt to hang Jay Lynch was unsuccessful as he fell to the ground.

When the second and final attempt was completed, the crowd, which included women and children, roared its approval.

The body hung from the elm tree on the north side of the courthouse for several hours before a Joplin undertaker cut it down.

Lamar funeral homes wanted nothing to do with Jay Lynch.

Among the people who stood on the Courthouse lawn as Jay Lynch met his fate was Arthur Aull.

Aull had seen the men preparing to storm the courtroom and had done nothing. He watched, absorbing and later reporting every grim detail of the death of the man who murdered Sheriff John Harlow and Dick Harlow.

He knew who the ringleaders were and while he wrote a lengthy, descriptive account of that day, he never wrote a word

The rope that was used to hang Jay Lynch in 1919 is on display in the Barton County Historical Society Museum in the basement of the Barton County Courthouse. *Photo by Randy Turner*

that would give a clue was to which people took the law into their own hands.

Whether that was because he knew the sentiments of Lamar residents were with those who practiced vigilante justice that night or whether he agreed with them, whatever the reason, the identities of the people who planned and executed the hanging of Jay Lynch, reportedly including prominent Lamar residents, remained unknown as Aull never put the names in print.

A quarter of a century later, another sheriff and his son had been murdered.

Would the killers of Roy and Sammie Patterson meet the same fate as Jay Lynch?

The coroner's inquest into the murders of Barton County Sheriff Roy Patterson and Sammie Patterson had just begun at River Funeral Home the afternoon of Friday, August 18, and the first witness had been called when a message was delivered to Coroner Raymond River that he was needed at the scene of an accident just past the railroad tracks on the eastern edge of the Lamar city limits.

When he arrived, River found the lifeless body of five-year-old Bonnie Kay Millard on the street by Brasher's filling station, which was owned by Bonnie's grandparents, Mr. and Mrs. J. E. Brasher.

Bonnie had been playing with two other children when she wandered into the road and was struck by a car driven by a man who had become distracted when he saw a pretty girl in another car.

The man was not driving fast, according to witnesses, but the girl was instantly killed.

The coroner's inquest resumed when River returned with witnesses including Sheriff Patterson's widow, Ira Farmer who discovered the bodies, the doctor who performed the autopsies and interim Sheriff Joshua Box.

Two witnesses who had been scheduled to testify, 16-year-old waitress Lilly Bemis and night attendant Pearce Hastings from Hite's Phillips 66 in Jasper did not testify.

Bemis and Hastings were in Skiatook, Oklahoma, to identify two suspects who had been taken into custody. The men, along with another man, had escaped from an Oklahoma prison and fit the descriptions of the men suspected of robbing

Hite's and killing the sheriff and his son. The other man had been captured and was being held in another location.

Not unexpectedly, when the hearing was completed, River determined the killers had stood at the south side of the car and shot Sheriff Patterson and Sammie and that the two men had been murdered.

It was a long day for Raymond River with the inquest and the child's death and it was not over yet.

It was that afternoon that the Chamber president learned Truman had accepted the invitation he and Mayor Guy Ross had extended to open his campaign in Lamar.

It was going to be a big day for the city.

River went home exhausted, but comforted by the news that Truman was coming, which would surely provide an emotional lift to a city that desperately needed it and that the killers of Sheriff Patterson and his son were safely behind bars.

River was unaware that Lilly Bemis and Pearce Hastings told Skiatook authorities that the jail escapees they had in custody were not the men who robbed Hite's.

The killers were still at large.

CHAPTER SIXTEEN

Now that their long shot invitation to Senator Truman to launch his campaign in Lamar had paid off, Mayor Guy Ross, Lamar Chamber President Raymond River and city officials faced the daunting prospect of having less than two weeks to prepare the city for the biggest event in its history.

A planning meeting was hastily scheduled at Memorial Hall and more than 200 gathered in the auditorium as River, Ross and the other members of the executive committee Rubey Ryder and William Lowrey conducted the meeting.

Options for a location for the Truman speech were debated. Lamar was justly proud of its city park and the Lamar High School football field had a flood lighting system that would be useful, but the only place that would offer enough space and access was the square.

The Truman event would be held on the west side of the Barton County Courthouse with a specially built platform over the steps for the speakers.

Committees were appointed, with all leadership roles being given to men, with the exception of the Ladies Committee, which would serve to greet and entertain the women in the

Truman entourage, a group that was expected to include Truman's wife Bess, his daughter Margaret, his 92-year-old mother Mattie Truman and his sister Mary Truman.

Carl Konantz was selected to head the Food and Drink Committee, even though it was well understood that the women would prepare all of the food. It was determined that the food stands would be situated just off the four corners of the square and that only Barton County church groups, clubs and organizations would be allowed to operate stands.

As the committee began work immediately after the public meeting, Konantz strongly recommended that each of the food stands serve fried chicken sandwiches, since they could "get a good stiff price" for them.

Also attending the Memorial Hall planning session were Jasper County Democratic Chairman Harry Easley of Webb City, a good friend of Truman's, who the Democratic National Committee had selected to serve as the state chairman for what was being called the "notification ceremony" and Joplin Chamber of Commerce Secretary Charley Hays.

Hays said the notification ceremony promised to be "the greatest event in southwest Missouri history" and pledged Joplin would help Lamar in any way it could, including financially.

The cooperation of surrounding communities was vital for Lamar officials if they hoped to pull off the Truman visit.

It would not be long, however, before city officials and Arthur Aull began wondering if the folks from Joplin had ulterior motives.

A few hundred people gathered at Lake Cemetery in Lamar Heights, just west of the Lamar city limits the afternoon of Tuesday, August 22.

The graves of many of those connected to the rich history of the city were located in Lake Cemetery.

It was the final resting place for the *Lamar Democrat*'s first editor Lee Chiswell, the stillborn first child of John and Martha Truman and Dr. W. L. Griffin, who was there when the Truman baby was born and then on May 8, 1884, delivered the man who had just received the vice presidential nomination of the Democratic Party

In 1919, the remains of Barton County Sheriff John Harlow and his son Dick Harlow were buried there and in a short time another sheriff and his son would join the number of those spending eternity in the placid grounds of Lake Cemetery.

Some of those who gathered near the area where earth had been moved only a few hours before to prepare for the arrival of Roy and Sammie Patterson had bypassed the Pattersons' funeral, which was held at Memorial Hall, while others left early to avoid being a part of the procession.

Though Memorial Hall was a large building for a city the size of Lamar, it was inadequate to handle the size of the crowds who came to pay their last respects to the sheriff and his son.

In addition to the hundreds who squeezed into the building, at least 200 more stood on the grounds, waiting to enter in sections to offer condolences to Mrs. Patterson and other family members.

The caskets sat end to end at the foot of the stage in the Memorial Hall auditorium with American flags draped over them.

The back wall and the sides of the stage were covered with

flowers. An honor guard from the American Legion post stood ramrod straight behind the caskets during the entire two-hour ceremony.

The Forest Grove Quartet consisting of Frank Lee, Glenn Brown, Floyd Joyce and Charles Quillin, whose son Donald had been killed in France 10 days earlier, sang two hymns, "Where They Never Grow Old" and "Going Down the Valley," accompanied by Dimple Haddock on piano.

Cecil Laster delivered the sermon reminding the mourners that they never knew when their day would come and that they needed to make sure they were ready for that day.

Each section of the overflow crowd walked through Memorial Hall, viewed the caskets and consoled the family,

"I can still see those two caskets there," Hannah Oeltjen said, more than 75 years after she crossed the Memorial Hall stage.

It was the first time I had ever seen a corpse," she said. "It was kind of scary for a five-year-old."

After everyone had viewed the caskets, they were carried to two River Funeral Home hearses and the procession to Lake Cemetery began.

It was a beautiful ceremony those who attended said when it was over, though that was something that was said after every funeral.

Two respected citizens had been murdered, their killers were still on the loose and Lamar boys were fighting overseas, with no guarantee they would ever return to their loved ones.

There could not have been a better time for the kind of welcome distraction that Harry Truman's nomination ceremony would provide.

CHAPTER SEVENTEEN

Simple logistics made it necessary that many of the activities surrounding Senator Truman's notification ceremony be held in Joplin, approximately 40 miles from Lamar.

A city of 3,000 did not have enough hotel rooms or dining facilities to be able to handle the number of radio, newspaper and wire service reporters, as well as national and regional Democratic political officials who planned to be at the Lamar ceremony.

From the beginning, Arthur Aull and city officials feared Joplin would steal Lamar's thunder and attempt to steer all activities to its hotels and restaurants.

There was no doubt Joplin officials intended to make Truman's stop as eventful as possible since it would bring considerable cash into the city's economy.

The Joplin Chamber of Commerce was heavily involved in the planning, but Chamber President George A. Spiva assured any Republicans who might not be happy with the organization throwing itself wholeheartedly into a Democratic Party political event that it was a matter of courtesy and the Chamber was only helping its neighbor to the north.

Initial events planned in Joplin included a dinner Wednesday, August 30, at the Conner Hotel, where Truman and his party would stay overnight, breakfast and lunch at the Conner and a trip to Camp Crowder approximately 20 miles away in Neosho in the afternoon before the contingent left to spend a few hours in Lamar before the evening activities.

Reading the reports in Joplin's morning and afternoon newspapers, the *Joplin Globe* and the *Joplin News Herald,* the extent of Joplin's participation angered Lamar officials who expressed their displeasure, both in the pages of the *Democrat* and by phone.

Chamber President Raymond River, upset with what he saw as Joplin's attempt to steal Lamar's thunder, made it clear in a phone call to Democratic National Committee secretary Bill Boyle, who was in Kansas City, something that upset River even more since Boyle had said he was going to be in Lamar.

According to Arthur Aull's account, River said, "You want to have the affair at Joplin, bring Truman up, have a few minutes, put on a brief ceremony and leave for Joplin again.

"If you are going to do that, just hold your darned meeting on some street corner in Joplin."

Whether River actually said those words remains in doubt, but Joplin's plans hardly changed at all, except that Bess and Margaret Truman had decided to come to Lamar the day of the event rather than going to Joplin the evening before.

The Joplin newspapers did not have to wait long to get back at Aull and Lamar city leaders for the way their city was being criticized.

∞

One day remained before what was being called Truman Day in Lamar.

"For Truman Day, get your hats, your horns and noise makers at Barry's Sporting Goods Store," an ad in the *Democrat* read and many Lamar residents were doing just that.

Decorations were being placed around the square, but as the morning turned into the afternoon on Wednesday, August 30, the storm clouds arrived and a steady rain began falling that continued the rest of the day.

Forecasters expected more rain was on its way for Thursday, threatening the biggest event in Lamar history.

The speaker's platform had been built over the steps on the west side of the courthouse, but city officials worried that their efforts could all be washed away.

H. C. and Pearl Chancellor had heard nothing further from the War Department since they received the letter notifying them that Richard was once again missing in action.

They threw themselves into their work preparing for Truman Day.

A friend of Richard's, Captain Jack Ryan, wrote H. C. Chancellor and attempted to boost his spirits.

Since I am a fond friend of Richard, your son, the letter telling me you'd received a notice of his being missing in action was quite a shock.

When I left for the states the 18th of July, Richard had around 28 completed missions. He was completely cured from his nervousness and had taken a position in the squadron as flight leader, which means he would lead a group of six to 12 planes.

I do not know where your son was forced down, but I assure you, Mr. Chancellor, that he, better than anyone I know, will be able to provide for himself.

The situation in Europe now is when our fighting men are forced down anywhere, with the exception of Germany proper, the chances are better than ever that they will be picked up by friendly natives.

Richard studied those locations and you can be rest assured that if it was at all possible, he is in friendly hands.

While the letter provided comfort, as did a visit from Richard's friend, Joe Young, the bombardier who had been with him the first time he was missing in action, the Chancellors continued to wait anxiously for some word, any scrap of information about what happened to their son.

They wondered if they would ever see him again.

OO

When Richard Chancellor returned to duty after his visit home shortly after the bombing of Pearl Harbor, the fetching high school girl his nephew had introduced to him, Ione Williams, was never far from his mind and he always kept her photo in his billfold.

When they initially parted, Ione returned to her studies at Marceline High School, where her everyday activities were much the same as they had always been.

It was her senior year and she was one of several girls at her school who were corresponding with soldiers.

"But none of them were going to get married," she said. At that point, it all seemed like more of a dream to her, but as time passed, she looked forward to receiving his letters more and more as they became an important part of each day.

While the letters were censored by the War Department to make sure no information was given on troop locations or that any military secrets were inadvertently included, Richard and Ione found a way for him to reveal information the department would not approve.

"We had a code," Ione said, describing a simple method Richard employed using first letters in sentences to spell out his location so she would know where he was.

During the time Richard was back on furlough after his initial missing in action experience in the Mediterranean, he had taken her to meet his parents.

At that point, the only mention of marriage had come from Richard's nephew, but Richard and Ione had developed something of an understanding.

It did not hurt that H. C. and Pearl Chancellor quickly grew fond of Ione.

After she graduated, she remained in Marceline, waiting for the war to end and reading Richard's letters.

Then they stopped coming.

More than anything, Ione wanted to see another one of his letters.

While the letters stopped coming to Ione Williams, Betty Gilkey, still a newlywed when her husband Gerald, after being drafted into the Army Air Force, was shipped to the Aleutians, was doing her part to help the war effort.

Betty moved from Sheldon to Kansas City, where she was worked for North America Aviation.

"I wasn't a Rosie the Riveter," Betty said, "I worked in the offices, but I knew all of those girls. I talked to them every day."

While Gerald Gilkey was far from the battle, he and the men who were in the Aleutians encountered a different kind of problem being stationed far away from home in a place where you were not going to get a two-week furlough to see the home folk.

Gilkey used a special talent to land one of the better jobs at his base, office manager.

""He was one of the fastest typists they had," Gilkey's son Steve said, "so they put him in the office."

While some men were unable to cope with the isolation of the base, Gilkey had two hobbies to help him pass the time photography and cutting hair.

At that point in their lives, neither Gerald nor Betty Gilkey gave much thought to the City of Lamar. It was a place where young people from Sheldon gathered on Friday and Saturday nights.

Lamar was a part of their past and would soon be a big part of their future.

CHAPTER EIGHTEEN

In its final article before Senator Truman arrived in Lamar, the *Joplin Globe*, in its Thursday, August 31, 1944 edition showed a markedly different approach in the way its reporter wrote about Lamar.

In previous days, the reporting had been straightforward and detailed the city's preparations for the arrival of what some estimates were saying could be as many as 20,000 people.

The article addressed the problems that an inch and half of rain and forecasts for more were causing Lamar officials and made a point of writing that the people who were hanging decorations around the square to celebrate Truman were all people "who do not know him."

As a contrast, in the same newspaper, a *Globe* reporter noted that Truman's face was "wreathed with smiles" when he arrived in Joplin the previous evening and rather than a group of people "who do not know him," the senator was greeted by "many old friends."

The article noted that Truman said he felt as if he had come home.

After establishing that Truman saw Joplin as a home, the

article took subtle, and some not so subtle, shots at Lamar.

The *Globe* reporter wrote of the small house where the senator was born six decades earlier, now the residence of Judge Walter Earp, and cast doubt about whether it really was the place where Truman was born.

"Nobody knows for certain," the reporter wrote, "because the Trumans were only here for four years."

Part of the blame for that might have rested on the shoulders of *Democrat* Editor Arthur Aull, who cast doubt about the Earp home being the house where Truman was born.

Aull printed speculation a few weeks earlier by someone who claimed Truman was actually born somewhere else, despite the fact that Truman himself and Mattie Truman had both vouched for the Earp home's authenticity during the 1934 Senatorial campaign, something which had been reported in the *Democrat* and Lamar old timers had taken him to the old Truman place during his 1924 visit.

Aull later declared definitively well before the *Globe* article was published that there was no doubt that the Earp home on Kentucky Avenue was Truman's birthplace.

The biggest insult in the *Globe* article was not the questioning of the Truman Birthplace authenticity, but the barely hidden insinuation that Joplin residents fully understood the importance of the Truman visit, but Lamar residents were hicks who lacked Joplin's sophistication and understanding of national politics.

The local population frankly admitted if there was any great excitement about tomorrow's show, it was centered as much in the national press and radio attention received as in the Truman visit.

Nowhere did the reporter give any indication of which

members of the "local population" had given him the impression, but while the glamour of having the national media coming to a city of 3,000 was undeniable and definitely drew the locals' interest, adults in Lamar, most of them avid readers of Aull's *Lamar Democrat* and the competing *Lamar Republican* (and even the *Joplin Globe*) fully understood the import of the Democratic national campaign being launched in the Barton County seat and the vice presidential nominee coming from their city.

More than anything, the Globe reporter's writing seemed to be the newspaper's response to Aull's criticism of Joplin trying to steal the event from Lamar.

The Globe's reaction was understandable.

It wasn't just Arthur Aull's criticism. Because of Aull's national reputation for his colorful prose and because reporters love a good controversy, the wire services picked up on Aull's criticism of Joplin.

The United Press reporter used the conflict in the lead of his article.

Citizens of Lamar have two worries today. The skies are heavy with precipitation and Lamar still thinks that nearby and bigger Joplin is trying to steal the Harry S Truman notification ceremonies or at least the bulk of them.

Reporters from the local, regional and national press filled the Conner Hotel in Joplin and crowded around Senator Truman and his contingent when they arrived from Kansas City Wednesday, August 30.

Truman did not offer the reporters anything newsworthy,

only repeating his assertion from earlier in the month that he would speak at Lamar and then deliver a Labor Day speech in Detroit.

Truman said he hoped for a "vigorous" campaign, but not an intensive one.

"After all, I still am a United States senator and I have work to do in the Senate. I shall continue to work at that job."

An informal dinner planned by the Joplin hosts was held that evening in the Empire Ballroom of the Connor, with another breakfast at that location the morning of Thursday, August 31, provided by Truman and the Democratic National Committee.

Among those attending was a Congressional contingent, consisting of 24 U. S. senators and four members of the House of Representatives that arrived at the Frisco Depot on the 6:30 a.m. train.

During a press conference at the Connor Hotel, Truman made a statement that in the 21st Century would have gone viral when he said, "An early end of the European War and resultant production cutbacks and unemployment would hurt the Democratic party's chances of victory in November."

No one appears to have been surprised by Truman's statement, which indicated the Democrats might need the war to continue, and of course, more lives of young soldiers lost, in order to win the election.

Truman immediately added, "However, I don't care what happens along that line. I want the war to end as quickly as possible. I'm thinking about those boys who are doing the fighting."

That would have been an excellent place to end the quote, but Truman was not finished.

"Unemployment always hurts the party in power."

In the modern era with representatives from the opposition party following the candidates, the beginning of the statement and perhaps the end would be used in campaign advertising while Truman's qualifying statement would be on the cutting room floor.

As it was, while Truman's comments were printed by the wire services they made little impression and were not featured in the headlines.

It was a case of the plainspoken senator presenting facts.

The entire quote was used and everything was kept in its proper context.

A reporter asked Truman what he would be saying in his speech later that evening in Lamar. He said he would "stick to the facts.

"However, the facts will include plenty of reasons why the Democrats should be re-elected."

Truman, the Congressional contingent, Joplin Chamber of Commerce President George A. Spiva, Jasper County Democratic Chairman Paul Van Pool and Harry Easley of Webb City, who was serving as the state coordinator for the Truman visit, took a motorcade about 20 miles south of Joplin to visit the troops at Camp Crowder just outside of Neosho at the invitation of Post Commandant Gen. Walter E. Prosser.

Prosser and Brigadier General Charles M. Milliken greeted Truman at the gate.

Camp Crowder was one of many bases constructed during the buildup to war in 1941. Truman's visit occurred on the third anniversary of the groundbreaking for the camp on August 30, 1941. Construction began immediately and it was completed just in time. Five days after the camp opened, the

Japanese launched the attack on Pearl Harbor.

The camp was named for Gen. Enoch Herbert Crowder, the Missouri native who authored the Selective Service Act, which was critical to the U. S. during World War I and then administered it.

The Neosho location was chosen because of its proximity to the conjunction of the Frisco and Kansas City Southern railroads, as well as its location near U. S. highways 66 and 71.

The camp, though it was initially intended as a place to train infantry, served primarily as the largest training center in the country for the Army Signal Corps, but it also served other purposes, including housing German and Italian prisoners of war.

Though it provided an economic boon to Neosho, a city of approximately 5,000, it was also virtually a city in its own right, featuring a hospital, post office, five theaters showing first-run movies, a radio broadcasting station, a camp newspaper and venues for entertainers.

The visit of another politician did not necessarily create excitement at Camp Crowder, though the men had the base in tip-top shape for Truman's visit.

The soldiers had seen politicians before and while there was a definite excitement about seeing the man who could become the next vice president of the United States, it was not quite the same level of enthusiasm as had been generated by the visit of movie star Cary Grant or the "King of Swing," jazz clarinetist Benny Goodman, heavyweight boxing champion Joe Louis or for that matter, the female singers and dancers in the frequent USO shows.

Among those stationed at Camp Crowder were cartoonist Mort Walker, who later used it as the inspiration for his syn-

Harry Truman is greeted by soldiers from Camp Crowder in Neosho on August 31, 1944. *Photo courtesy of Truman Library and Museum*

dicated comic strip "Beetle Bailey," and actor/writer/producer Carl Reiner, who used his own experiences there as the inspiration for flashback episodes of the 1960s television situation comedy he created, *The Dick Van Dyke Show*.

Truman was shown a large portion of the camp, though

it was impossible to see even half of it since Camp Crowder covered 43,000 acres.

Truman spoke with dozens of soldiers, asking about their work and their families and left many of the men with the impression they were talking to someone who was more like a grandfather than a person who could be a heartbeat away from the presidency.

After having a meal with the soldiers, Truman and his entourage left Camp Crowder to begin the 60-mile trek to Lamar.

CHAPTER NINETEEN

—— ⊙⊙ ——

The traffic was nearly always brisk at the Travelers Hotel, but it was even more so on Truman Day.

H. C. Chancellor's hotel was not only located in prime real estate, just a half-block south of the square and a half block from Highway 160, but it also been designated as a hub of activity for Truman's visit.

Five-year-old Hannah Fry knew every corner of the Travelers Hotel.

It was her home.

The hotel featured a dining room with white tablecloths and white napkins with three-course meals. The dishes were cleared between courses.

The hotel also had a beauty shop that Hannah's mother, Lucille Fry, operated. The family lived in an apartment at the Travelers Hotel and the staff all knew Hannah, who often accompanied the cleaning ladies as they made their rounds.

Staff members enjoyed their work and enjoyed working for Chancellor.

"I knew all of the Chancellors," Hannah said. "They were wonderful people."

Travelers Hotel in the 1940s. *Photo courtesy of the Barton County Historical Society*

The Travelers had been a fixture in Lamar long before Chancellor bought it in 1932, though not always under that name.

It opened as the McMillen Hotel during the Christmas holiday season in 1897. Within a year, it sold and became the Jackson Hotel, which remained the name until 1916, when the hotel sold. After another sale two years later, the name was changed to the Hotel Travelers and eventually modified to Travelers Hotel.

Upon entering the hotel, a visitor's attention was immediately captured by the chandeliers that brought a touch of glamour to the hotel and the long, winding staircase that led to the upper floors.

"The staircase was huge," Hannah said. "Of course, I was a small child, so everything was huge."

Out-of-towners coming to hear Roosevelt's vice presidential candidate speak began filling up the Travelers the previous evening and even more arrived the morning of Truman Day.

When they walked into the hotel, if their attention was not captured by the elegance of the lobby, visitors quickly noticed the prominent posters of Franklin D. Roosevelt and the man who had become Lamar's most famous native son.

The stormy weather that had dumped an inch and a half of rain on Lamar the previous day had disappeared. Not only did it appear the rain would not return on Truman Day, but there wasn't a cloud in the sky.

The square was roped off with no traffic allowed except delivery trucks.

Sandwich stands were set up just off the square on each corner, while churches also served as dining halls for the throngs of visitors who poured into the city.

With wartime gasoline rationing in place, rides were shared from nearby communities and by some attending from hundreds of miles away.

The 30x50 foot platform where Truman would speak was in place at the west steps of the Barton County Courthouse.

Banners were hung around the square. The National Democratic Committee had paid for $1,500 worth of decorations.

The railway stations were also decorated so that anyone arriving for the Truman speech would know they were attending a political event.

The Palace Drug Store was turned into headquarters for the state, regional, and national press with Arthur Aull and his daughter, Madeleine Aull VanHafften, serving as hosts.

The wives and daughters of visiting dignitaries were greeted at the Travelers Hotel by a welcoming committee, consisting

of Goldia Ross, Mayor Guy Ross' wife; Pearl Chancellor, Luanna Aull, Mrs. Ed Stephens and Ila Gathman, wife of Lamar
City Councilman Loyd Gathman.

Harry Truman's wife Bess and their daughter Margaret
were among those welcomed by the committee.

Bess and Margaret Truman at the Democratic National Convention in
Chicago in July 1944. *Photo courtesy of Truman Library and Museum*

According to some wire service and national newspaper accounts, Bess and Margaret Truman had their first opportunity
to look at the house where Harry Truman was born.

The *Lamar Democrat*, however, printed a letter to the editor from James H. Lillard of Lamar, who said he had been
introduced to Truman, during his 1934 Senatorial campaign

and the senator was accompanied by Bess, Margaret and by Truman's mother, Martha Ellis Young Truman.

We escorted him to what is now the Walter Earp home on East Eleventh Street and Kentucky Avenue. Judge Truman's mother recognized it as her former home.

In the biography Margaret Truman wrote about her father in 1972, she made her disdain for spending August 31, 1944 in Lamar clear.

It was a day to remember – or forget – depending on your point of view.

That, unfortunately, was about the nicest thing Truman's daughter had to say about the city where her father was born.

After describing the huge crowd who came to see Truman, Margaret Truman criticized the city.

One thing was certain. It (the notification ceremony) was too big for Lamar. Toilet facilities and the sewage system broke down. The parking field was turned into a huge mud hole by a heavy rainstorm the previous day. Poor Harry Easley, who was the chairman in charge of the day, almost went crazy.

"All I can say," he muttered, summing it up, "is never have a big affair in a small town."

So she would not be bored while she was in Lamar, the women's welcoming committee had two local teenagers provide a tour of the city to the 20-year-old Margaret.

As unimpressed as she was with the City of Lamar, the teenage girls were equally unimpressed with Margaret Truman, pegging her as a snob after spending the afternoon with her.

As the day wore on, it was time for Truman to arrive and just as quickly that time passed.

There was no sign of Harry Truman.

○○

The failure of the Truman party to arrive on time made it difficult for Arthur Aull, who hoped to have coverage of the guest of honor's arrival in time for the afternoon paper.

Aull waited until the last possible moment before typing his story and then handing it to the linotype operator. He described the crowd that awaited Truman at the Travelers Hotel.

They were all awaiting the arrival of the Truman party and the parade to come and it was late. It was scheduled to arrive at two o'clock, but it looked as if it would arrive at about four.

All the time the town was filling up. It was plain that this process would go on all evening. The crowd was even getting larger and it was be a fine and gala night for old Lamar.

CHAPTER TWENTY

—— ∞ ——

As H. C. and Pearl Chancellor threw themselves into Truman Day activities, every once in a while keeping thoughts of their missing son from their minds for a few brief moments, on that same day a letter was written to H. C. from the War Department, which he did not receive until later that week.

Dear Mr. Chancellor:

I am writing you with reference to your son, Richard Chancellor, who was reported by the Adjutant General as missing in action over Yugoslavia since July 22.

Further information has been received which indicates that Lieutenant Chancellor was a crew member of a B-24 Liberator bomber which departed from Italy on a bombardment mission to Ploets, Rumania on July 22.

Details are not available, the report indicating that while returning from the mission, your son's bomber was seen to drop out of formation at about 2:25 p.m. and to lose altitude.

This Liberator was last seen as the formation neared the coast of Yugoslavia, flying toward Italy.

Inasmuch as the crew members of other planes on this mission were unable to make further observations of this aircraft, the above facts constitute all the information presently available.

Please be assured that a continuing search by land, sea and air is being made to discover the whereabouts of our missing personnel.

As our armies advance over enemy territory, special troops are assigned to this task and all agencies of the government in every country are constantly sending in details which aid us in bringing additional information to you.

∞

Not everyone who descended upon Lamar for Truman Day came to see the vice presidential candidate or to participate in a major social event, which it certainly was.

With the crowds came people looking to make some quick and easy money.

At least four people were victims of pickpockets and those were just the ones that Arthur Aull found out about and dutifully reported in the pages of the *Democrat*.

Willis Dearing reported losing $15 to $20, while Mel Ridgely had $17.50 stolen, George Kaderly $500 in cash and checks and Jim Schubert was touched for an unknown amount.

In addition to the pickpockets, Lamar found itself besieged by what Aull described as "smooth looking operators, teams of "crapshooters' that were preying on men who let their guards down with just a bit of encouragement.

"They enticed their victims into games with a drink," Aull wrote.

And there were plenty of drinks available in Lamar that day. Mayor Guy Ross reported 20,000 bottles of beer had been shipped to the city's three taverns.

∞

Harry Truman and the traveling party of national and state officials arrived in Lamar two hours later than expected, but the late arrival failed to dampen anyone's enthusiasm.

They drove into a city where the Lamar High School Band greeted them. The streets were lined with signs of support for the Roosevelt-Truman ticket and banners proclaiming "Welcome Home, Harry."

Seven marching bands, including bands from Springfield, Joplin and Carthage, in addition to the Lamar High School Band, played patriotic tunes to usher the senator into the city.

Mayor Ross and the welcoming committee greeted Truman and the other visitors. Following a parade and a concert featuring the local and visiting bands, an informal reception was held at the Travelers Hotel, followed by a banquet at 5 p.m. at Memorial Hall.

Another band concert entertained the people who gathered on the Lamar Square at 7 p.m. as thousands waited to hear from the vice presidential candidate.

Through it all, Truman smiled and enjoyed his interactions with Lamar residents and others who had come to the city. While some of the dignitaries tried to keep Truman to themselves, he was having none of it.

While Truman had little connection to Lamar other than the happenstance of birth, he enjoyed retail politics and meeting and talking with Missourians.

Many of those who were attending were farmers and Truman, from experience, knew just how hard they worked and how much their contributions made to the state and to the country.

Truman was also familiar with the business owners and the people who worked for them. His brief conversations with the people were not filled with political platitudes. Truman talked to them and, more importantly, he listened.

That was something even a member of the Republican Party like Mayor Guy Ross, who accompanied him everywhere he went that afternoon and evening, recognized.

Ross had known Truman slightly during World War I. The artillery company Truman commanded was located next to Ross' company.

"I knew him, but he probably didn't know me," Ross recalled 50 years later. "I do know that he would take off his shirt at night and come on down to the back of the barracks and shoot craps with the boys."

Despite his 10 years in the nation's capital and his status as the man who very well could be elected vice president of the United States in three months, the Harry Truman Guy Ross met that day was the same man Ross remembered from the war.

"He was a real nice fella all the way around," Ross said.

In addition to Senator Truman and the elected officials and party leaders who accompanied him from Joplin to Lamar, another party of VIPs arrived in Lamar just before the official notification program began.

It was the first time Martha Ellen Young Truman had been in the city where she gave birth to a son on May 8, 1884 in 10 years.

The 92-year-old broke her hip in the spring of 1944 and her vision was almost completely gone, but she did not intend to miss one of the biggest moments in her son's life.

Harry Truman and his mother, Martha Ellen Young Truman in 1944.
Photo courtesy of Truman Library and Museum

Maj. Gen. Ralph Truman, Harry Truman's cousin, drove Mattie Truman and her daughter Mary Jane, who lived with her in Independence, into the city. It had been arranged for the car to be allowed onto the square and an area had been set aside directly by the speaker's platform.

She would not be able to see her son, but she would have no problem hearing every word.

OO

A meal honoring Truman was held at at the Connor Hotel in Joplin August 30, 1944. *Photo courtesy of Truman Library and Museum*

Many of those who milled about the Lamar square settled into the spots where they planned to watch the evening's festivities. They had patronized the various organizations' food stands and had picnic lunches on or around the courthouse lawn, complete with fried chicken or fried chicken sandwiches and fresh homemade cherry pie, washed down by iced water or tea.

Few of them had ever seen the spectacle of the national media, at least as it was constituted in 1944, descending on a community.

Watching the major radio networks set up their equipment in preparation of broadcasting the event to the nation was nearly as fascinating as the circumstances that brought them all together.

The wire services were represented, as were major regional

newspapers, including the *Kansas City Times*, *Kansas City Star*, *St. Louis Star and Times* and the *St. Louis Post-Dispatch*. The Lamar area newspapers, including the *Joplin Globe* and *Joplin News-Herald* were represented, all checking in from time to time in the makeshift press headquarters that had been established in the pharmacy building.

Playing host to them and thriving in the attention his city was receiving was Arthur Aull, probably the only Lamar resident who had ever drawn the attention of the national press, but that attention had been nothing like this.

Among those who chronicled Harry Truman's return to home to accept the vice presidential nomination was the veteran national reporter for the *New York Times* Turner Catledge, an accomplished journalist who later became the newspaper's first executive editor.

They sat among the elms in the courthouse yard under as beautiful a full moon as ever shone in these parts.

Catledge estimated the crowd at 7,000, though other estimates ranged from 10,000 to 20,000. Truman's speech, however, would reach far beyond those who were standing shoulder to shoulder or who were seated on the courthouse lawn.

The national radio audience reached millions, Catledge noted.

It was a national radio audience that almost did not happen.

What made Truman's August 31, 1944 speech historical was its launch of the national presidential campaign, but the networks had to be convinced the speech needed to be covered.

At the Republican Convention, the networks carried a complete speech, amounting to 30 minutes of broadcast time, from the vice presidential candidate Ohio Gov. John Bricker.

Truman did not make a long speech at the Democratic

National Convention, only taking enough time to thank the delegates.

J. Leonard Reinsch, who scheduled radio time for the national ticket, dealt with network officials who felt they complied with equal time requirements when they broadcasted Truman's brief thank you. If Truman wanted the airtime, they contended, he should have talked longer.

Reinsch was finally able to convince the networks to give Truman the time. After that, he began to work on the senator's presentation.

Obviously, the first problem was to slow the candidate down in his delivery, and second, to bring more emphasis to the important points and make a better radio presentation than is normally the case with someone with the Midwestern twang, or a Missouri twang, whatever you want to call it," Reinsch remembered.

Truman still kept rushing through his practice sessions until Reinsch devised a plan.

I started the idea of putting less and less material on each page, so he would have to turn pages frequently. The turning of the pages would take time and the mechanical process would slow down his delivery.

Reinsch's methods were nowhere near perfected when Truman made the notification acceptance speech.

"The Lamar speech was a real headache," Reinsch said.

The cause of that headache was not Truman, but the powerful Texas senator who was introducing him.

After a morning and early afternoon of socializing and an afternoon of lip smacking meals, parades and band concerts, it was time for the main event.

Those accustomed to the raucous political rallies of the 21st Century would have a hard time recognizing their 1944 counterparts.

In this era before the advent of rock music, when country music was still referred to as country western, the only introductory music before a political event such as the notification was the playing of the National Anthem.

The style of dress for Truman Day was anything but casual. The men were dressed in their Sunday best, though in a nod to the August heat, dispensed with jackets.

The women were not only wearing their finest dresses, but were also sporting new hats, many of them provided over the last few days during the various Truman Day sales.

The welcome to this purely Democratic Party event was held on a speaker's platform dwarfed by huge likenesses of President Roosevelt and Truman was given by Lamar's Republican mayor Guy Ross, who then introduced Sam Weir, the Democratic state chairman.

Rev. Cecil Lasley gave the invocation.

The next portion of the program featured the introduction of various dignitaries, including state officials and a host of Truman's fellow Senators including Tom Connolly of Texas, Joseph Guffey of Pennsylvania, Carl A. Hatch of New Mexico, John L. McClellan of Arkansas, Ernest W. McFarland of Arizona, Elmer Thomas of Oklahoma, Claude Pepper of Florida and D. W. Clark of Idaho.

One who had been scheduled to be in Lamar, but had to cancel at the last moment was Sen. A. B. "Happy" Chandler of Kentucky, who later became the commissioner of Major League Baseball.

Sen. John L McClellan informed the audience the event they were attending was "the official opening of the national Democratic presidential campaign."

National radio coverage did not begin until the notification address given by Sen. Connally of Texas, who was known to be one of the great orators of the United States Senate, began.

The Connally speech was a cause of great consternation for J. Leonard Reinsch. In his deals with the networks, he had only received 30 minutes of broadcast time, but the stem-winding Connally had a much longer speech than Reinsch preferred.

"Senator Connally's introduction was a long speech in itself which got me upset."

After discussing the situation with Connally, the speech was reworked to about 10 minutes, but after Truman's team thought the revisions had been completed, Connally began adding material.

During his speech, Connally, the chairman of the powerful Foreign Relations Committee, spelled out the theme of the campaign.

The American people will not place in untried hands the military and naval leadership upon which depends not alone the security of the United States, but the survival of liberty in the world.

The American people will not cashier the commander in chief of the Army and the Navy on the field of battle.

In the next portion of his address, Connally offered a look at the future beyond the world war when nations would work together.

The people of the United States will not summon the President of the United States away from the council tables where, with our allies, is being erected a world organization to preserve the peace and to chain aggressors who would again plunge the earth

Harry Truman and Sen. Tom Connally of Texas in Lamar on August 31, 1944. *Photo courtesy of Truman Library and Museum*

in blood.

Connally lived up to his reputation as a powerful orator. Party officials were initially concerned that the Texas senator would overshadow Truman, a capable, but far less gifted speaker, but finally figured correctly, that the community's good will for their native son would enable them to overlook any such considerations.

As Connally, whose style of bombastic oration, would seem out of place in 21st Century politics, concluded his speech, Truman, wearing a tan suit and looking more like a banker or an insurance salesman than a man who might possibly be the next vice president of the United States, stepped onto the platform, drawing heavy applause from the mass of people on the Lamar Square.

Truman's message echoed what Connally said- it would be a mistake to change the commander in chief when the nation was at war and there was no one who could steer this country to victory any better than Franklin D. Roosevelt.

Truman opened with a formal acknowledgment of the purpose of his appearance. "Mr. Chairman, members of the Notification Committee and fellow citizens, I am deeply honored to have been named as the Democratic Party's candidate for the vice presidency and accept with humility and a prayer for guidance that I may perform honorably and well whatever tasks are laid before me."

Truman reached for a glass of water that had been placed on the lectern, took a drink and then returned to his address.

The vice presidential candidate wasted no time steering his speech to its theme, punctuating his main points most often by jabbing his right hand forward, the index finger pointing outward and occasionally by thrusting both hands forward.

"Franklin Delano Roosevelt is my leader and commander in chief," Truman said and the crowd began applauding.

"In the past, I have supported the policies formulated by him to protect and advance the welfare of our nation. I will continue to do so and will continue my efforts to make certain that those policies are carried out promptly and efficiently by those entrusted with their administration."

While Truman did not have the trained voice of a public speaker, he was addressing a hometown community that did not have anyone who had not been affected by the war.

Truman Day had begun as a celebration of the hometown boy (though only for 10 months) who was making Lamar proud. As Truman continued with his speech, it became a call for the people of Lamar and southwest Missouri to support the continuation of the Roosevelt presidency and keep a steady, sure hand at the helm.

We have long been engaged in a desperate struggle to preserve our liberties and to safeguard the American way of life. Many of our brave citizens have given their lives to win for us the certainty of victory, now assured.

All of us now toil and sacrifice to win this most terrible of all wars. Victory is now in sight. Our courageous, well trained and completely equipped soldiers and sailors are beating down the enemy wherever he can be found. Their unequaled valor under the greatest leadership ever given a fighting force guarantees the victory.

From her seat in a car parked to the side of the speakers' platform, Mattie Truman nodded approvingly as her son delivered the most important speech of his life, just four blocks from the small house on Kentucky Avenue where she had given birth to him 60 years earlier.

As much as she had always supported the political career of Harry Truman, she also supported President Roosevelt and the Democratic Party.

Truman noted that the task would not be completed even when victory was won on the field of battle.

When victory is won, government must provide for our returning veterans and our war workers an assurance that their sacrifices were not in vain, that they will return to a country worth fighting for, that they will have the opportunity to earn a good living and that the same humane principles and policies for the protection of the average man and woman carried out under Franklin D. Roosevelt for the past 12 years will be continued under his leadership.

Truman praised the efforts of U. S. soldiers and sailors and said those efforts and Roosevelt's leadership put the Allies on the brink of winning the war, but the victory still must be won.

"Military victory over Germany is but a step", Truman said, noting that after that the U. S. had to triumph over Japan and then prepare for the new world that would emerge from those victories.

War has taught us, whether we like it or not, we cannot build a wall of isolation around the United States. Our very existence depends upon the establishment and maintenance of a sound and just peace throughout the world.

Truman's speech, interrupted frequently by applause, was not a collection of platitudes or lines guaranteed to garner the audience's approval. It was substantive, despite the limited amount of network radio time he was allotted, even addressing such areas as the failure of President Woodrow Wilson's League of Nations following World War I, to the effectiveness of the Lend-Lease program through which the U. S. supplied weapons to those fighting Germany even before the U. S. entered the war in December 1941.

Another reason to keep Roosevelt in the White House, Truman said, was the amount of time it would take for a new president to get up to speed.

It takes time for anyone to familiarize himself with a new job. That is particularly true of the President of the United States, the most and difficult complex job in the world.

Even in peacetime, it is well recognized that it takes a new president at least a year to learn the fundamentals of the job. We cannot expect any man wholly inexperienced in national and international affairs to readily learn the views, the objectives and the inner thoughts of such divergent personalities as those dom-

inant leaders who have guided the destinies of our courageous allies.

There will be no time to learn and once mistakes are made, they cannot be unmade.

Senator Truman would find out just how true those words were in coming months when he would be he, and not Gov. Dewey, who would be placed in that position.

Truman concluded his acceptance speech by stressing once more the importance of re-electing Roosevelt.

The welfare of this nation and its future, as well as the peace of the whole world, depends upon your decision on November 7.

You can't afford to take a chance. You should endorse tried and experienced leadership- you should re-elect Franklin D. Roosevelt president of the United States.

During those last words, Truman gestured with both hands, leaning over the lectern. When his final words were spoken, those on the speakers' platform stood and led the crowd in applause with Sen. Connally raising both hands above his head.

Truman reached for his glass of water.

An eagle-eyed wire service reporter, noticing the senator's 92-year-old mother in the back seat of the car parked alongside the platform approached her, joined by a couple of other reporters who did not want to miss out on anything.

Mattie Truman told the reporter she had not minded the long trip "I think it would have been worth coming from California to hear."

The proud mother added, "There isn't a finer man living than Harry Truman."

The biggest speech of Truman's life came in the city where she had given birth to him and she had been there to hear it.

It was the last visit Mattie Truman ever made to Lamar.

∞

It did not take long for the excitement and glamour of Truman Day to evaporate, replaced by the grim reality of war.

While victory was at hand in Europe, the troops were still at risk.

On September 12, less than two weeks after Truman Day, 62 Barton County boys took the bus to Fort Leavenworth to be inducted.

Three days later, Arthur Aull wrote of the death of another Lamar soldier.

Word came Tuesday morning from the War Department that Corporal Dean Duvall, son of Mr. and Mrs. Leroy Duvall and a member of the United States Marines serving in the Pacific, had been killed in action.

He was an outstanding boy and one who would attract attention wherever he went.

He was a volunteer in his country's service and a very willing and eager one.

Corporal Duvall's survivors, Aull wrote, included his brother Darryl Duvall, a paratrooper who had been injured in a jump recently.

Another brother was also in the service.

Lamar residents did not have to be reminded that the United States was still a nation at war.

CHAPTER TWENTY-ONE

During the return trip after flying a successful mission July 22, 1944, the engines on Lt. Richard Chancellor's bomber was struck by ground fire forcing him to make a crash landing in Yugoslavia.

Though Chancellor and his crew survived, Chancellor suffered a severely broken arm, as well as other minor injuries. His men sustained cuts and bruises.

Within a short time, they were taken prisoner and transported to Sarajevo. From there, they were taken to Stalag Luft III in Poland, a POW camp for captured airmen.

Chancellor arrived at Stalag Luft III four months after 76 prisoners escaped in what was memorialized in a book by former POW Paul Brickhill and a later Hollywood movie starring Steve McQueen, James Garner and an all-star international cast as *The Great Escape.*

Of the 76 men, only three succeeded in reaching freedom. Hitler, angered by the embarrassing escape, had 50 of the recaptured prisoners executed in violation of the Geneva Convention.

The other 23 prisoners were returned to the POW camp.

Before the escape, Stalag Luft III was considered to be almost impossible to escape because of the extra precautions the Germans had taken.

The barracks were built two feet off the ground to make it easier to detect any tunnels and the land that was selected for the camp featured soil that had more of the consistency of sand making it more difficult to dig tunnels.

Strategically placed seismographic microphones enabled the guards to hear any digging or other unusual sounds.

After the "great escape," the guards' vigilance increased even more, not wanting to suffer any further embarrassment.

That was the situation Chancellor and his men walked into when they arrived at the camp.

The camp had five compounds, with each compound consisting of 15 single-story buildings, each measuring 10 x 12 feet with enough room to house 15 men who slept in five triple-deck bunk beds.

The officers, including Chancellor, were housed in separate buildings from the other airmen.

The camp eventually held approximately 7,500 U. S. airmen and 2,500 from the Royal Air Force.

Eight hundred Luftwaffe guards, most of them either too old to serve on the front lines or rehabilitating from being injured in battle, were in charge of the prisoners.

For months after the camp opened in March 1942, prisoners were restricted in the type of news they received and heard only of great German victories and how the Germans were easily winning the war.

That changed after a British prisoner managed to be brought into camp with copper wires hidden on his person. Using the wires and more than a little ingenuity, the men were able to create a makeshift radio and pick up BBC broadcasts.

The radio was kept hidden in an accordion.

While the airmen were treated far better by their Luftwaffe guards than those held in other prisons, life was still difficult.

The meals varied little and offered almost no nutritional value, usually "a daily portion of German bread and cabbage soup," Chancellor said.

A loaf of bread weighed four pounds and often the prisoners received only 1/12 of a loaf.

Though the cabbage soup's taste was not unpleasant, it came nowhere near to meeting the prisoners' appetite and often, it came garnished, unintentionally, with fresh maggots.

In addition to the hunger, Chancellor had to deal with the effects of his broken shoulder.

The camp had doctors, but these were not men who had ever dealt with the kind of complex fracture Chancellor suffered.

As one operation failed, the doctors tried another and Chancellor, having heard the stories of Nazi atrocities, was left to wonder what was being done to him.

"Richard thought the doctors were conducting experiments on him," Ione Chancellor recalled.

While these doctors were not would-be Mengeles, they also were not equipped to handle Chancellor's injury and left him in constant pain.

Truman was not the only vice presidential candidate to speak in Lamar.

New York Gov. Thomas Dewey's running mate, Gov. John Bricker of Ohio, made a 15-minute speech from the platform of a railroad car in the hometown of his vice presidential opponent October 27.

The stop was one of several Bricker made en route to Joplin. He started his day with a speech in Harrisonville, then addressed crowds at Rich Hill and Nevada before arriving in Barton County.

At each location, Bricker hammered the New Deal and stressed what a Dewey Administration could do for Missouri and the nation.

Bricker said the Republican Party planned to help small businesses by "eliminating excessive and repressive regulations," and accused the Democrats of having Communist leanings.

"When our boys come home," he said, "they don't want to come home to the communists who are running the Democratic Party."

Bricker did not mention Truman.

The crowd was estimated at 1,500 according to the *Joplin Globe* and 2,500 according to the *Joplin News Herald*.

Bricker was greeted by a patriotic selection from the Lamar High School Band. Barton County Republicans presented Mrs. Bricker with a large bouquet of flowers.

○○

The biggest event in Barton County political history had taken place August 31 when Harry S Truman accepted the Democratic vice presidential nomination at the steps of the courthouse.

That was not enough to stem the Republican tide that swept through the county Tuesday, November 7.

Roosevelt-Truman 1944 Campaign Poster. *Courtesy of Truman Library and Museum*

Not only did the Dewey-Bricker ticket defeat Roosevelt-Truman, but the final result was not close.

Dewey received 3,190 votes to 2,511 for Roosevelt.

Senator Truman awaited the election returns with friends at a suite in the Muehlebach Hotel in Kansas City.

When a radio announcer commented early in the evening that Missouri might go Republican, Truman said, "I think this calls for a concert," and motioned for the crowd to follow him to the grand piano in the suite.

"(Truman) amazed the group with a professional-like rendition of Paderewski's difficult "Minuet," a United Press reporter wrote.

When he had completed the piece and the applause stopped, the senator said, "Gentlemen, I wish I had stayed with music," paused for dramatic effect and added, "along with politics."

The announcer turned out to be mistaken in his assessment. The Roosevelt-Truman ticket won Missouri's vote as well as the national vote.

When election night ended, Roosevelt was elected by an Electoral College landslide 432-99.

The baby that Dr. William L. Griffin had brought into the world 60 years ago in Lamar was the vice president-elect of the United States.

CHAPTER TWENTY-TWO

Only one southwest Missourian, Webb City banker Harry Easley, was in the audience January 20, 1945 in the south portico of the White House to see Harry Truman officially become vice president.

Two days earlier, Truman resigned as a U. S. senator in preparation for his new position.

The ceremony lacked the pomp and circumstance of previous inaugurations due to the war. Two American flags and the military honor guards provided the only color.

Truman wore a dark topcoat and held his hat in his hand as he swore to uphold the Constitution.

After Roosevelt was sworn in for his fourth term, he delivered a brief 551-word speech, saying, "In the days and years that are to come, we shall work for a just and durable peace as today we work and fight for total victory in war."

An audience of 7,806 attended, according to a White House count.

Two days later, Truman returned to the U S. Senate, this time to preside. As he stepped into the chamber, his former colleagues began applauding.

Truman brought the session to order by banging a cherry wood gavel that had been given to him by Missouri friends.

In the audience for his big moment were his wife Bess, daughter Margaret and a contingent of about 75 Missourians, including Easley.

As the first day ended, a reporter asked Truman what kind of vice president did he intend to be.

"I have worked hard all my life," Truman said. "That's the only recipe for success I know. I'm going to be the hardest working vice president you ever saw."

With the exception of his botched surgeries at the hand of German doctors, Richard Chancellor's first months at Stalag Luft III were uneventful.

He had heard stories of atrocities the Germans had inflicted on their prisoners, but that was not the experience he had, though it was by no means an easy existence.

"You would be cold outside and know that it would be cold inside the barracks- cold at night when you went to bed and the same the next morning."

It was an experience the airmen lived through day after day.

At Stalag Luft III, Chancellor said, the commandant attempted to abide by the Geneva Convention. "The guards were all old men," he said, ranging in age from 55 to 68.

While strong leadership among the prisoners helped keep their morale steady, even more helpful was the news they were hearing about the war.

"We knew the war was coming to a close through the radio

broadcasts."

As the calendar turned to 1945 the POWS, through their makeshift radios, heard BBC reports on the continued victories of Allied forces.

As the allies neared Stalag Luft III, the Nazis took quick, decisive steps.

When the camp was liberated in January 1945, Chancellor was no longer there as he began the first of two forced marches. During the marches, the airmen not only had to deal with the bitter winter cold, but risked death from friendly fire from Allied bombers.

During one such instance, Chancellor found himself dodging bullets. He dived into a trench to avoid the bombs and found himself with another prisoner, a young man named Bill Goade.

The two men struck up a conversation as they waited for the raid to end.

"Where are you from?" Chancellor asked.

"A little place you've never heard of," Goade said. "Duenweg, Missouri."

Chancellor chuckled even as the bombs were flying and he told Goade he was from Lamar.

Duenweg, a community of 2,000, was three miles east of Joplin and only about 40 miles from Lamar.

In a trench thousands of miles from home in this God-forsaken area two southwest Missouri men had been thrown together.

CHAPTER TWENTY-THREE

Since her return to Lamar in 1942, Madeleine Aull Van-Hafften had done everything she could to make the burden of running the *Democrat* easier for her father and in exchange Arthur Aull provided her with a graduate course in how to run his type of small town newspaper.

As 1945 began, Aull was 72 years old and had been the editor of the *Democrat* for more than 44 years, but his health was continuing to fail and he began turning more and more of his duties over to his daughter.

Time had taken its toll on his vision, as well. Aull had so much more he wanted to accomplish and he continued to love his work, but he knew his time was nearing an end.

The invasion of the national reporters into his city a few months earlier with Aull playing host to them showed him an existence that might have been his if he had made other choices.

"Arthur had many opportunities to go to large city papers," his wife Luanna Aull said. "I can recall many interviews with newspaper and magazine representatives, but he was never tempted. He wanted to be his own boss, to say what he thought was best for his community and his country.'

It had been months since Truman Day, but the national media maintained an interest in the vice president's hometown. The interest extended to its colorful newspaper editor.

The national attention Aull received when syndicated columnists reprinted his colorful accounts of Lamar news was nothing compared to what he was about to receive.

In his twilight years, the spotlight was about to shine on Arthur Aull.

∞

The February 26, 1945 issue of *Life Magazine* featured a cover photo of an American soldier, one of those fighting on the western front in the battle against Germany, with the article inside referring to the men as "winter soldiers."

Since *Time* Publisher Henry Luce bought the rights in 1936 to the name of what had been a humor magazine, *Life* had grown into the most successful magazine in the United States, selling more than 13 millions copies a week.

Luce's idea was to tell stories in photos, accompanied by short articles in comparison to the deep reads that were provided in his other magazines, *Time and Fortune*.

It was an immediate hit.

The February 26 issue featured its usual combination of photo features on the war, domestic politics, world politics and U. S. events and included one photo taken February 10 that created a sensation.

In her biography of her father, Margaret Truman wrote about the photo of her father and rising movie star Lauren Bacall, 20, who had made a sensational film debut as a teenager the year before alongside Humphrey Bogart in *To Have and Have Not.*

During the war, the National Press Club opened its doors to serviceman on Saturday and provided them with free hot dogs and beer. Bacall showed up as a welcome surprise to the approximately 800 soldiers.

Truman had also been invited.

One invitation my father regretted accepting was to a National Press Club party. Someone asked him to play the piano and he cheerfully obliged.

Actress Lauren Bacall, also a guest, climbed onto the top of the upright and gave him one of her sultriest stares.

Dad, sensing trouble, tried to look the other way, giving the impression that he was playing from sheet music that was somewhere off to his left. But he was trapped between his instinctive politeness, which made it impossible for him to hurt Miss Bacall's feelings, and his equally instinctive political awareness that he was flirting, not with Miss Bacall, but with trouble.

Margaret explained that Bacall was only doing what her press agent had told her to do, but that did not make the photo a hit with the Truman family.

Mother did not care for it much. She thought it made Dad look undignified and much too carefree for the vice president of a nation at war.

Another Truman biographer, David McCulloch, indicates Bess Truman's reaction was stronger than what her daughter described.

Bess was furious. She told him he should play the piano in public no more.

Truman was not the only person connected to Lamar who was featured in that issue of *Life.*

On page eight, the week's "Life Reports" article was head-lined in bold capital letters, AULL PRINTS ALL THE NEWS with a smaller subhead reading "Fearless Missouri editor gives the human touch."

In his lead, the writer, John R. Cauley, explained the essence of Arthur Aull's brand of small town journalism.

Arthur Aull, editor and owner of the Lamar, MO Democrat for 44 years, operated on the simple theory that the function of a newspaper is to print all the news.

Unlike most country editors whose papers reflect their own native caution and orthodoxy, Editor Aull believes it is his duty to tell literally everything that happens in his town. So far, Mr. Aull has been sued three times, unsuccessfully, and assaulted only once.

Cauley provided several samples of Aull's warts-and-all reporting and described how he did not subscribe to any wire services, but wrote the contents of the *Democrat* each day himself, except for the women's news and club news, which his wife Luanna wrote.

The *Life* article provided a complete news story Aull had written about the kind of event that would never make it into the pages of almost any other newspaper in the nation.

At 7:30 p.m. Monday, an 8-½ pound son was born to Miss Jennie Wirts, bookkeeper for the Lamar Trust. At 9 o'clock, Don O'Neal, cashier of the bank, stood by her bed and they were married by the Rev. Martin Pope.

Miss Jennie had been at her work in the bank every day until Monday when she was detained by symptoms she did not understand. No one in the bank who daily worked side by side with her suspected she was in a condition of expectant motherhood.

This included the cashier, Don O'Neal, the father of the child.

The bride is 33, the groom 53.

None of the folks at the bank where Miss Jennie worked day after day suspected. There apparently wasn't a whisper from the sharp-eyed gossips.

Mr. O'Neal was plainly taken by complete surprise, but he never wavered in his decision to make no attempt to concealment or evasion.

Don and Jennie, fine couple that they are, will stand forth soon with their little son- secure as ever in public esteem.

We could have said they were married secretly, say a year or two ago, Don told a friend, but it wasn't that way and we're not going to lie.

Well, true enough, there never was a better girl than Jennie and we all know Don is a grand old boy, but God, it was badly managed.

Aull told Cauley his purpose was to set the record straight and stop lies from spreading through gossip.

With its circulation of more than 13 million, the issue of *Life Magazine* caused the Harry Truman/Lauren Bacall photo and to a lesser extent the legend of Arthur Aull to "go viral" in a day decades before that phrase was created.

Aull, next to Pulitzer Prize winning Emporia, Kansas editor William Allen White, was the most well known small town newspaper editor in the nation.

In a couple of months even more attention would come Aull's way.

While the *Lamar Democrat* did not have daily reports from Associated Press and United Press to keep readers up to date on the latest news on the war in Europe or in the Pacific,

Arthur Aull provided them with something even better.

At least two or three times a week during the war years, Aull featured letters from soldiers who knew they could talk directly to all of their loved ones and friends by sending letters to the newspaper.

When he did not receive letters from soldiers, he was still able to offer updates on how they were doing through conversations with their parents and news items sent to him by the War Department.

Each time another group of draftees left for induction, Aull reported details, including the names of all of those making the trip.

In the March 23, 1945 *Democrat*, Aull printed a letter from Lamar boy Bud Moore with the dateline "Somewhere in France."

There is still a long way to go and Germany is like a writhing snake, very deadly as long as there is life at all.

With Hitler and his fanatical followers still at the helm, they will fight on to the bitter end and I am afraid that end is still quite a distance off even with our hammer-like blows and bigger ones to come.

People seem to have forgotten that while England, France and the United States were sleeping, Germany was preparing for all of this and her one big mistake was that she did not build a big enough navy for had she done this England would surely have been defeated and we would have had a long old war to face with no end in sight.

Moore wrote of one day in Paris when he ran into three other Lamar soldiers, Wally Konantz, Vern Bickel and Jack Reavley.

From one o'clock in the afternoon until ten that night we dis-

cussed many things but the principal one was of home and how anxious we were to get back there.

A drive through France convinced Moore how much of a recovery the French would have in store when the war ended.

At least the Americans are going to have a complete country to come home to, with no bombed out homes and businesses and farmers spending part of their time filling up gaping holes in the ground and your loved ones being spared from death or injury from all kinds of war.

Yes, when victory comes, it will be cheap at whatever price it costs for God has spared our country from all of these horrors.

CHAPTER TWENTY-FOUR

Vice President Truman was at the Capitol the afternoon of April 12, 1945 when he received word from Steve Early, the president's press secretary, that he was needed at the White House.

When Truman arrived, he was immediately escorted to First Lady Eleanor Roosevelt's second floor suite, where Mrs. Roosevelt, Early, and the Roosevelts' daughter and son-in-law, Anna and John Boettiger, were waiting.

"Harry, the President is dead," Mrs. Roosevelt said.

Truman was stunned, but after a long pause said, "Is there anything I can do for you?"

"Is there anything I can do for you?" she responded. "For you are the one who is in trouble now."

Chief Justice Harlan F. Stone of the Supreme Court was called as were members of the Cabinet and Congressional leaders and told to come to the White House. Calls also went to Bess Truman and to the media.

A red-tinged Bible was found belonging to an usher and when everyone was gathered, the Chief Justice began administering the oath of office, with Truman holding the Bible in his left hand and raising his right hand.

"I Harry Shippe Truman," Chief Justice Stone began.

"I Harry S. Truman," he corrected and moments later, the son of a mule trader became the 33rd president of the United States.

It was just before five o'clock in Lamar when President Roosevelt's death was announced.

The skies, already darkened from cloud coverage, soon released a torrent of rain on the city, something Arthur Aull noted in the *Democrat*.

Here in Lamar, a few moments after the news had flashed over the radio, the rain began to fall.

The very skies wept and mingled their tears with those which fell from the eyes of the people.

Aull offered praise for Roosevelt's guidance of a nation at war.

No one can deny that he got us through the worst and led us on to triumph.

He not only got us through the worst, but he left a vice president who was eager to carry out Mr. Roosevelt's wishes.

The first full day of Harry S Truman's presidency, Friday, April 13, 1945, was an eventful one, as the new commander in chief held a 20-minute meeting with Secretary of State Edward Stettinius, met with Congressional leaders on Capitol Hill and issued a proclamation declaring Saturday, April 14 as a day of mourning for President Roosevelt.

"Though his voice is silent, his courage is not spent, his faith is not extinguished," the proclamation read.

"The courage of great men outlives them to become the courage of their people and the peoples of the world.

"It lives beyond them and upholds their purpose and brings their hopes to pass."

Truman met with the cabinet and afterward Secretary of War Henry Stimson told him of the existence of a powerful new weapon. Though Stimson provided few details, he asked Truman not to look any further into it because the project could be ruined if its existence became public.

Through his work with the Truman Committee, the president had an inkling that was something was going on because of large amounts of money that were being poured into the locations where work was being done on the Manhattan Project with no explanation.

Stimson's words were the first time Truman had heard of the weapon that would lead him to make one of the most monumental decisions of his presidency.

Martha Ellen Truman, 93, was unable to be in Washington to see her son sworn in as president, but she listened to his speech on the radio and later when it was in print, had her daughter Mary Jane read it to her.

"I heard every word he said," she told a *New York Times* reporter. "Harry's going to be all right. Everyone who knows him at all and heard him this morning knows he's sincere.

"He'll do what's best."

Later that day, the phone rang and Mrs. Truman was told the White House was calling. She talked briefly with her son, telling him she had listened to his speech.

The conversation ended with her telling Harry Truman the same thing she told him time after time through his childhood.

"Now you be a good boy, Harry."

Martha Truman lived long enough to see her son reach the White House and spent time there, though she always preferred her Missouri home.

If she was in awe of the White House, she never showed it. With memories of raiders running her family out of her home and burning it in the 1860s, she wanted nothing to do with her son's offer to sleep in the Lincoln bedroom.

She said she would never sleep in a bed where "that man" slept.

Feisty and active until the end, Mattie Truman died at her home in Grandview July 26, 1947, four months shy of her 95th birthday.

∞

After Truman declared April 14 a day of mourning, Lamar Mayor Guy Ross followed suit.

Shortly after word of Roosevelt's death was announced, Lamar officials and ministers began considering a memorial service in his honor to be held 1 p.m. Saturday at Memorial Hall.

Though no official announcement was made, word circulated throughout the community and when the time for the service arrived, more than 200 gathered at Memorial Hall.

As part of Mayor Ross' proclamation, all businesses on the

square were closed between 1 p.m. and 1:30 p.m.

Flags were flown half-staff in honor of Roosevelt through-out the city.

The ceremony included brief messages from four ministers, the reading of an obituary for Roosevelt, reading of scriptures and a group rendition of "America."

With all of the attention naturally focused on the death of the man who had been president since 1933, the thoughts of Lamar residents now turned to the man who replaced Roos-evelt at the helm.

As hard as it was for them to believe, someone who had born in their city was now the president of the United States.

It was not Roosevelt's death or the ascension of Truman that most occupied the mind of H. C. Chancellor.

The Travelers Hotel owner had not heard a word from the Department of War since the October letter telling him it had been confirmed that his son Richard was a prisoner of war.

Lt. Col. Dave Craig, who knew Richard and had previ-ously written to Chancellor offering words of encouragement, mailed a letter to him April 13.

The war situation looks a lot better from both fronts now so perhaps it won't be so long.

I hope this big drive into Germany succeeds and that it will succeed in reaching some of the P. W. camps. I know you're anx-ious about Richard and are hoping for his early release.

Since I started writing this, the radio just flashed the news of the death of Roosevelt. That wasn't so unexpected by those close to the President, but nevertheless, it was a great blow.

I know of no man who could have handled the job of the past four years and the future years of this war as well as he. He will go down in history as another Washington and Lincoln.

While Truman may not be of presidential stature, I feel confident that he will be as good as any available under present circumstances. He's well schooled in rough and tumble politics and that's what it's going to take.

Chancellor's hopes for his son's release received a boost on Tuesday, May 8, 1945, Harry Truman's 61st birthday, as Germany formally surrendered.

The war in Europe was officially over.

The wait for news of Richard's fate continued.

∞

A V-E day service was held 9 a.m. May 8 at Memorial Hall, one hour after Truman's official proclamation.

Some businesses closed for the service, others, following Truman's request that business continue as usual, stayed open, but allowed any employees who wished to attend the service to do so.

When the *Democrat* was published that afternoon, Arthur Aull connected the national story to the city he had called home for 45 years.

Sixty-one years ago today, May 8, 1884, Harry Truman was born in a small frame cottage in the city of Lamar. Today, May 8, 1945, he is President of the United States and the people listened as he delivered his V-E Day proclamation.

Lamar, like most other towns, was more or less worn out on V-E Day, but the people listened joyously to the president as he proclaimed the final and official announcement of victory in

Europe.

Three weeks later, a telegram arrived from the War Department with the news H. C. and Pearl Chancellor had waited months to hear- Richard had been freed from the POW camp and was back in the states.

After he and his fellow prisoners were freed from the Germans, they were provided large amounts of malted milk to gradually prepare them for a regular diet.

In the weeks after his liberation in early May, Chancellor gained 20 pounds.

On June 2, the Chancellors were reunited with their son.

While it was a joyous occasion for the family, there was one more reunion Richard Chancellor was anxiously anticipating.

Ione Williams had been in his thoughts every day during his captivity and in the years since he had last laid eyes on her.

Now Chancellor would be able to see her again and she could provide the answer to the question that continued to linger in his mind.

Had she been waiting for him?

There was no flashy, emotional scene when Richard Chancellor and Ione Williams saw each other, but to them it was something that was much better.

It was as if no time had passed at all and they were just as comfortable with each other as they had been before Richard went overseas.

Ione and Richard Chancellor in the early 1940s. *Photo courtesy of Ione Chancellor*

Over a long dinner, they shared their plans for their future, their hopes, their dreams, their ambitions until Richard looked at Ione and said thoughtfully, "I think this is going to work."

Ione understood exactly what he was saying. She knew him well enough to know that in that brief understatement, Richard Chancellor had just proposed to her.

With equally few words, she agreed with his assessment of their situation and soon after planning began for a wedding.

On June 23, 1945, in the H. C. Chancellor home at 209 S. Gulf Street in Lamar, Ione and Richard exchanged vows.

Seventy-four years later, seated in her living room, Ione Chancellor looks at the corner of the room.

"We were married right there," she said and more than seven decades later, she lives with a daily reminder of one of the happiest moments of her life.

CHAPTER TWENTY-FIVE

After V-E Day, the war in the Pacific continued, but at long last there was a feeling on the home front that the time of praying each day that the news will not feature the death of a friend or loved one was coming to an end.

Lamar had put its best foot forward in supporting the war effort since December 7, 1941, complying without complaint to rationing, flying American flags, planting victory gardens, writing letters to soldiers and sailors and continuing to send off the young men of the community as they boarded buses and headed toward their inductions.

Now the people of Lamar and Barton County had a chance to breathe and begin the process of putting the war behind them, something they would never be completely able to accomplish.

Part of that process was the memorial service May 29 at Memorial Hall for the 53 young men from Barton County who had given their lives for their country.

Seven hundred fifty people sat shoulder to shoulder and lined the walls of the auditorium for the program, which had been arranged by the American Legion posts in Lamar and

Liberal.

The ceremony began with the entire audience joining to sing "The Star Spangled Banner," followed by the invocation given by Rev. S. M. Connell of the Catholic Church.

Rev. Frank B. James delivered the address, followed by the most solemn portion of the ceremony- the reading of the roll of the 53 casualties.

As each name was read, Joan Hays Bergwell, wearing the uniform of the American Nurses Corp, placed a carnation in a large vase.

Audible sobbing could be heard from different sections of the auditorium, especially from the area that had been reserved for approximately 250 family members of the deceased. Most of the tears, however, were shed silently.

As they departed Memorial Hall, the 750 shared one hope-that no one else would be added to the roll before the war came to its conclusion.

∞

Life Magazine brought more national attention to Lamar for a feature on "Harry Truman's Missouri" in its June 26, 1945 edition.

This time, Lamar shared the spotlight with Independence and Grandview, but the article still kept Lamar as an integral part of the new president's life story.

Lamar, the president's birthplace, is a typical county seat of 3,000 people with a big central Court House and a nationally famous small-town newspaper, the Lamar Democrat.

Some of the old timers there remember the president's father, John, as a wiry young man who joked a lot and knocked people's

Harry Truman talks with Judge Walter Earp in August 1944 in front of the home where Truman was born. *Photo courtesy of Truman Library and Museum*

hats off when they weren't looking. He was also one of the slickest mule traders Lamar ever saw.

The *Life* article contained inaccuracies, beginning with the concept that John Truman had been a slick mule trader when in fact, his business came nowhere near succeeding in Lamar.

The article also had Harry Truman spending the first few years of his life in Lamar, while he had not even made it to the one-year mark before the family headed north.

The article featured photos of Truman's birthplace, as well as its owner, Judge Walter Earp, showing him seated in a chair in the house reading a copy of the *Democrat*.

Earp was referred to as a "cousin and former deputy of Wyatt Earp, two-gun sheriff of Tombstone, who got his start in Lamar."

Another photo showed Judge Earp with his son Everett. The photo prominently showed a mule shoe that purportedly was the very one that John Truman nailed above the door after his son was born.

It strained credulity to think that a mule shoe placed by a previous owner of the Birthplace would still be in its original location or still located on the property nearly 40 years later when Judge Earp bought the house.

The *Life* reporter and photographer were among the first to contribute some of the lore that has been built around the day Truman was born.

Though the house was still there, little else remained from May 8, 1884, so the stories began to grow and Everett Earp encouraged them.

Harry Truman was president and the younger Earp, who along with his brother, were once his father's deputies when Judge Earp was Barton County sheriff, saw an opportunity.

His father's home was no longer the birthplace of a senator or even a vice president.

Where others saw a small older house, Everett Earp not only had an appreciation of the house's significance, but a desire that it be recognized as a place of importance and if he made a dollar or two as a result, so much the better.

Earp's first opportunity came in July 1945 when three men from the History to Miniature Foundation came to Lamar.

The foundation created miniature replicas of presidential birthplaces and wanted to add Truman's birthplace to its list.

The foundation did not make a profit off its work and no one ever asked for money in exchange for access to the homes.

The Earps asked for $500.

They didn't receive a cent.

Foundation representatives set up across the street and used surveyor's instruments to take measurements, snapping photos from different angles.

When they completed their task, no one was able to tell that the Earps had not allowed them access to the property and Lamar received more national attention.

Madeleine Aull VanHafften had spent the past three years working closely with her father and enjoying sharing her father's passion of putting all of the news in the *Democrat*.

Her fervent hope was that she could continue to do so for years to come, but as the months passed she noted a continued deterioration of his health.

He could no longer see well enough to read and his daily sojourns to cover his beats were becoming more difficult. It was no longer a matter of if she would be taking over for her father. Now the question was when.

After a brief brush with fame in the 1930s and early 1940s, Harry Truman and *Life Magazine* made Aull a star, but he obviously was not going to have much more time to enjoy his newfound stardom.

Two more major stories remained for the *Lamar Democrat* editor and both of them came in the space of one event-filled week.

CHAPTER TWENTY-SIX

George Sylvester Huston was not surprised when his pool game at a Kansas City establishment was interrupted by police officers who arrested him July 29 for the August 17, 1944 murders and for the armed robbery of Hite's Phillips 66 in Jasper.

One of the two men who were with Huston that night, Victor Monroe Rush, 24, who went by his middle name, had been arrested during the past week in Dallas, Texas, where he had been living with his wife and three children.

The third man, Huston's younger brother, Ernest, was still at large.

The 37-year-old Huston, had been described as the leader of the gang, despite standing only five feet five inches tall and weighing less than 150 pounds.

Huston matched the description the filling station attendant Pearce Hastings and the teenage waitress Lily Bemis had given investigators.

Huston had a lengthy criminal record dating back to 1916, when he was placed in an Iowa reform facility at age 11 and spent several years in the Illinois state penitentiary in Joliet after being convicted of forgery.

When he was taken into the police station, Barton County Prosecuting Attorney Roth Faubion and Highway Patrol Trooper Chet Oliver were waiting to interrogate him.

At first, Huston denied any involvement with the robbery or murders, until Oliver produced a signed statement from Monroe Rush's father, Victor, a Kansas City resident.

Arthur Aull detailed the story in the *Democrat*.

The elder Rush told the officers along last fall that he and (Monroe) went to Richmond to visit with the boy's mother from whom his father is separated.

While there, the older Rush said that his son told them he and his two companions had been apprehended down near Lamar by the sheriff.

The sheriff had hauled the three out of their car and was making ready to get them to his own car to bring them to jail when he (Rush) made some sort of movement. He said the sheriff drew his gun and in his excitement shot and killed his own son.

This story, relayed to the officers by Rush's father, although a fantastic tale, was enough to convince the father that Rush had been in on the murder.

After that, authorities began searching for the Huston brothers and Rush and nearly caught one or more of them several times, but each time they were able to get away.

Dallas Police arrested Monroe Rush, who was living with his wife and three children and using the name Victor Strong.

Confronted with the evidence against him, George Huston admitted his involvement in the robbery and the murders of the Pattersons, but Faubion and Oliver were still not certain who fired the fatal shots.

It was the younger Huston brother who was the first to name a shooter when he was captured a couple of days later.

Robbery and murder were the furthest things from their minds the evening of August 17, 1944, Ernest Huston said.

The three men were looking for a house where George Huston and his wife could live and somehow the conversation turned from houses to the possibility of holding up a filling station.

"We pulled up to a filling station and all three of us got out of the car. Monroe told the station attendant to put in some gas. After the gas was in, George and Monroe pulled guns and told the attendant this was a stickup.

"George and Monroe took the money out of the register and out of the man's pockets. I took some cigarettes."

While Ernest Huston's confession did not quite match up with the robbery details they had learned from Hastings and did not even mention the teenage waitress Lily Bemis, there was enough truth to it that investigators believed his story.

After the robbery, the three men were returning to Kansas City when a car pulled alongside them and Sheriff Roy Patterson, who had been alerted to the robbery by Hastings, shouted for them to stop.

"We pulled up on the side of the road and the car stopped behind us. George and Monroe got out of the car and told me to hide. They went back to the other car and I crawled out into a ditch.

"I heard someone from the other car ask how many people were in our car and George and Monroe said 'just us.' They did some more talking and a short time later, I heard some shots. I don't know how many."

Huston said he had never been involved with anything like this before.

"I was scared and still am. The next thing I remember

George told me to get in the car so we could get out of there."

As they drove home, Huston said, his brother said they had to remove the motor number from the car so it couldn't be identified.

Using a tire tool and wrenches, the three men took turns trying to remove the number, but they were not entirely successful, so they poured gasoline on the car and set it on fire.

"After that, we left on foot through the woods. We rode freight trains and caught rides along the highway."

Two days later, they reached Kansas City. Huston told his wife what happened and she urged him to turn himself in. He had almost done so many times, he said, but each time he changed his mind at the last instant.

"Now I want to help the officers clean up this murder."

As Huston told his story at the Barton County Jail, word began to spread that one of the men who killed Sheriff Patterson and his son was in the jail and an angry crowd began to gather.

Fearful of a repeat of the hanging that ended the life of Jay Lynch killer of Sheriff John Harlow and his son Dick in 1919, deputies quietly spirited Huston out of the jail through a back entrance and took him to the Cedar County Jail in Stockton 39 miles east of Lamar.

Efforts were underway to get Monroe Rush extradited from Texas and George Huston was being held in the Newton County Jail in Neosho about 60 miles from Lamar.

The three men who had been involved in the robbery and murders had been captured.

That news brought the emotions of the previous year flooding back to Lamar and Barton County and made the grief and anger as fresh as if the murders had just taken place.

Word was circulating through Lamar that the same justice that Jay Lynch received 26 years earlier was the only way to avenge the deaths of John and Sammie Patterson.

CHAPTER TWENTY-SEVEN

The White House released President Truman's message 10 a.m. central time Monday, August 6, 1945:

Sixteen hours ago, an American airplane dropped one bomb on Hiroshima … It is an atomic bomb. It is a harnessing of the basic power of the universe.

We are now prepared to obliterate more rapidly and completely every productive enterprise the Japanese have above ground in any city.

We shall destroy their docks, their factories and their communications. Let there be no mistake; we shall completely destroy Japan's power to make war.

If they do not now accept our terms they may expect a rain of ruin from the air, the like of which has never been seen on this earth.

Truman was returning from meeting with England's prime minister, Winston Churchill and Russian Premier Joseph Stalin at the Potsdam Conference when he received official notification by dispatch that the bombing mission had been successful.

He shared the news with the men serving on the Augusta as he made his way home by sea.

"Keep your seat, gentlemen," Truman said, waving the dispatch. "I have an announcement for you.

"We have just dropped a bomb on Japan, which has more than 20,000 tons of TNT. It was an overwhelming success."

After the applause from men who realized that the end of the war was close to being a reality, Truman left to begin spreading the word to each area of the ship.

The word was spread across the nation with immediacy by radio and by special editions of newspapers, with the news of the atomic bomb spread across the top of page one in banner headlines with much larger font than usual.

The *New York Times* headline displayed in three lines across the top of page one read, "FIRST ATOMIC BOMB DROPPED ON JAPAN; MISSILE IS EQUAL TO 20,000 TONS OF TNT; TRUMAN WARNS FOE OF A 'RAIN OF RUIN' "

Southwest Missouri's leading afternoon newspaper, the *Joplin News Herald*, used bold capital letters at the top, as well as a term that while used commonly grew to be seen as a racist pejorative by later generations- "ATOMIC BOMB USED ON JAPS"

Eight days later, following a second atomic bomb dropped over Nagasaki, the Japanese surrendered.

Arthur Aull's *Lamar Democrat* did not exactly follow the lead of the *New York Times* or even the *Joplin News Herald* with its page one coverage of the end of the war.

Rather than a banner headline across the top of the page, Aull, who normally had one-column headlines written in bold capital letters, but the same size as the regular copy, made an exception for the momentous occasion and spread a headline over two columns- "A VICTORY NEVER BEFORE

EQUALED IN THE HISTORY OF THE WORLD."

At a time when people read and wrote far more voraciously than they do in the 21st Century, events like the dropping of the atomic bomb and the surrender of Japan spelled out the primary weakness of the *Lamar Democrat* as a daily newspaper.

As thoroughly as Aull covered local news and the tremendous flair he added in its telling, his coverage of the national news that affected Lamar and Barton County primarily came from his extensive reading and his rewording of material other people had written.

The *Democrat*, as one of the few daily newspapers in a city the size of Lamar, did not pay for wire coverage from Associated Press or United Press.

Readers who wanted more coverage of state, national and international news were forced to take a supplemental daily newspaper like the morning *Joplin Globe* or the evening *Joplin News-Herald*.

It did not help that Aull was no longer the Arthur Aull of even a few years earlier.

The deterioration began with a 1942 incident in which Aull was at the *Democrat* office when he suddenly found himself almost totally blind.

Aull attempted to drive home and instead veered into a parked car. It was the beginning stages of arteriosclerosis and though his vision improved and he kept working, by 1945, Madeleine was handling more than half of the stories.

Aull did not relinquish the major stories like the bombing of Japan to Madeleine.

And when it came to the big local stories such as the capture of the killers of Sheriff Patterson and his son, those were the ones that he was going to keep to himself.

CHAPTER TWENTY-EIGHT

A few weeks before the end of the war, Sgt. Gerald Gilkey received welcome news at the isolated outpost in the Aleutians. He was heading home.

Gilkey's furlough was approved, as was his request for it to last five weeks.

For the first time in three years he could return to Sheldon, his wife Betty and his family.

Gilkey enjoyed his work managing the supplies, but he had watched as the loneliness had taken its toll on many of those who served at the base.

Serving as the base barber helped Gilkey deal with the isolation, as well as providing him with extra money to send Betty. He also had thrown himself into photography, a pleasant productive way to pass the time.

But he was ready to go home.

It was not long after Gilkey arrived in Missouri that the news broke that the war was over and Gilkey learned that while his country appreciated his services, it did not need them any longer.

Gilkey's personal things remained at the Aleutian base.

"He never went back to pick up any of his belongings," Betty Gilkey said.

His son, Steve Gilkey added, "He didn't want to go back and get his stuff because he was afraid they'd hold him there."

The war was over, Gerald Gilkey was back in the states and now he had to figure out what he was going to do with his life as he began a path that eventually led him back to Lamar, the city where he once cruised the square in a canary yellow Model T dragging a burning tire behind him.

∞

The preliminary hearing for the accused killers of Sheriff Roy Patterson and Sammie Patterson, originally scheduled for August 7, was delayed until August 17 to give time for George and Ernest Huston to find lawyers who would represent them.

Ernest Huston and Monroe Rush were held in the Greene County Jail in Springfield while George Huston was in the Newton County Jail in Neosho.

Fearful of a recurrence of the events of a quarter of a century earlier when an angry mob dragged Jay Lynch out of the judge's chambers and hung him from an elm tree in the courthouse yard, the hearing was held three days earlier than it had been advertised.

Highway Patrol troopers were able to sneak the Huston brothers into the courthouse without the public knowing it. The judge, Barton County Prosecuting Attorney Roth Faubion, Special Prosecutor Lynn Ewing from Nevada and the lawyers were the only ones there as they waived their preliminary hearings, then were spirited out of the courtroom and returned to jail.

The hearing for Rush was delayed, but word spread that Rush had confessed to being the one who killed the Pattersons and said he had fired all of the shots, except one, which was fired by Sheriff Patterson.

On October 23, 1945, Monroe Rush, George Huston and Ernest Huston pleaded guilty to first-degree murder and were sentenced to life in prison.

The capture of those involved in the killing of Sheriff Patterson and his son and the events leading up to their guilty plea and sentence was the final major story in the career of Arthur Aull.

In early 1946, though Aull's name remained on the masthead and he remained publisher, the *Lamar Democrat* was in the hands of Madeleine Aull VanHafften.

Though there had never been a day while Aull was publisher that he did not have competition in the form of one daily newspaper or another, his sheer force of personality, the power of his writing and the audacity of the personal items he was willing to put into print kept his newspaper the number one news source in Lamar.

There were more than a few who thoroughly disliked Aull, but subscribed anyway because they did not want to miss the latest community scandals.

Another thing that kept the *Democrat* on top was Aull's keen business sense.

Though Madeleine learned a lot from her father, she did not have his knack for business.

It did not take long for the competition to notice.

∞

With the nation still engaged in a slow recovery from the Great Depression and fears rising throughout the nation that we would soon be at war, President Franklin D. Roosevelt declared Saturday, November 23, 1940 a general day of Thanksgiving.

That is exactly what it was for the many people who were involved in a brawl two days earlier during the traditional day of Thanksgiving in the United States.

One of those who had much to be thankful for was a Lamar High School freshman saxophonist who was involved in one of the few times when the band played a key role in a football brawl.

That budding musician was taller than most of his classmates and so slender it looked as if a stiff breeze would knock him to the ground.

That night, it came close to being a clenched fist.

The incident occurred during the most important football game of the year for Lamar fans, the traditional Silver Tiger battle between Lamar and Nevada, this time played on a frozen field in the Vernon County seat 25 miles north of Lamar.

Each year, the winner of the game took home the traveling trophy, the aforementioned Silver Tiger. The trophy was created in 1933 to symbolize the rivalry and during the first seven years Nevada won it five times, including 1938 and 1939, but even though Nevada did not win in 1934 or 1937, neither did Lamar, as each contest ended in a 7-7 tie.

Nearly half of Lamar crowded onto the visitors side of Nevada's field with a strong feeling that this was going to be the year the trophy could finally be placed in the spot that had been reserved for it in the high school's trophy case.

Of course, that was what Lamar fans thought the previous seven years, as well.

When Lamar took a 6-0 lead early in the second quarter, Lamar fans' hopes were stirred once more. After Nevada failed to move the ball, Lamar had an opportunity to increase its lead. That was when the on-field incident that sparked the brawl occurred.

That saxophonist, Marvin L. VanGilder, wrote about the incident 56 years later:

The Lamar quarterback threw a long, high pass that connected perfectly with the receiver, who leapt high into the air to receive the pigskin.

At the moment he grasped the ball, the receiver was hit simultaneously by two Nevada tacklers, one approaching from the front and the other from one side, a collision in mid-air. The impact flipped him abruptly flat onto the rock-hard turf and his head struck the surface with the force of a pile driver.

The Nevada fans rose en masse in their bleachers to scream their approval. But on the field, the Lamar Tiger lay quietly, an unmoving heap of grid gear and clothing.

Time passed as managers and coaches and volunteers from the stands labored over the fallen star. Then an ambulance was summoned, and still not moving, the pass receiver was placed on a stretcher and carried from the field.

The removal once again excited the Nevada fans, who rose to scream out their joy and denounce the fallen invader. That was a bit too much for the members of the Lamar High School Band.

We arose, leaving most of our instruments behind, and dashed across the frigid field, ignoring the protests of Director Kenneth

Fite, and lunged angrily at the mass of screeching fans in the Nevada stands.

Some other Lamar fans had joined us by the time we reached the offending cheering section and the result was a near riot, finally quelled through the combined efforts of coaches, other faculty members and a few other sensible adults from both sides of the field.

Most involved in the brief melee escaped with only bruises and scratches, but the Lamar pass receiver, as we later learned, was critically injured and faced a difficult period of hospitalization.

One bright spot- When the game ended with Lamar holding on for a 12-0 lead, the Silver Tiger was heading south for the first time.

Another bright spot- No one was arrested, including that saxophonist, who was no ordinary 14-year-old. As a high school freshman, VanGilder not only showed considerable skill as a musician, but also as a writer and a speaker, and he had already started a journalism career doing odd jobs and writing school news for Arthur Aull's competition, the *Lamar Republican.*

VanGilder described himself as a "green kid from the farm with an addiction to words and their potential."

VanGilder's daily duties, he recalled years later, included "melting buckets of lead atop a fiery red potbellied stove and pouring the contents into molds to form type and cut for illustrations and thereafter placing those products tediously by hand into metal forms, locking same in place and installing them on a flatbed press by feeding large single sheets of newsprint into its gaping receptacle."

After that chore was completed, VanGilder hand-folded each copy of the *Republican* as it left the press and, along with his brother, Charles VanGilder, delivered the newspapers to local subscribers.

VanGilder's reporting work was not limited to school coverage. His first feature story was an interview with *Republican* publisher Gaylord Heath about an activity he was coordinating for the Missouri State Fair.

The launch of his journalism career did not last long, as VanGilder's father took a job in Stockton shortly after the bombing of Pearl Harbor and then was transferred to El Dorado Springs where VanGilder graduated from high school in 1944.

Though VanGilder's first foray into the world of Lamar newspapers was brief, it was the beginning of a long distinctive journalism career and one that would bring him back to compete with the *Lamar Democrat* again.

CHAPTER TWENTY-NINE

When Franklin D. Roosevelt died and Harry Truman became president, the house where Truman was born was no longer just an old building, but a place of historical significance.

Everett Earp, who became owner of the house following the death of his father, Judge Walter Earp, on December 21, 1945, had big plans for the house.

"Everett was determined that the birthplace would become a monument to the president even though Truman had moved away when the baby was 11 months old," Earp's niece, Reba Earp Young, recalled.

While it was Earp's cousin, Wyatt Earp, who had become nationally known through movies and books, most recently in the 1946 movie *My Darling Clementine*, the highly fictionalized retelling of the 1881 shootout at the O. K. Corral in Tombstone, Arizona starring Henry Fonda as Wyatt Earp and Victor Mature as Doc Holliday, Everett Earp also had a reputation as a man who was capable with a gun.

Known as "Big Chief," Earp had a lengthy career in law enforcement, having the distinction of being Lamar's last constable, just as Wyatt had been the first and though the opportunities to use the skill were few and far between, Earp also had a reputation for having a quick draw.

Earp claimed the skill had been passed down through the Earp family and he passed it on to his son Roy, who later developed a reputation as the fastest draw in the Oakland, California Police Department and was profiled in the *Oakland Tribune.*

Everett Earp's law enforcement days were in the past and he saw an opportunity in owning the house where President Truman was born.

What would make it an even more valuable property would be if Truman were to somehow manage to be elected to a full term instead of just being someone who reached the high office of the land due to the death of his predecessor.

The prospect of Truman being elected seemed dim as 1948 arrived. Three years had passed and the glow of the final victory over the Axis powers had dimmed.

Truman's Democratic Party was fractured by defections of members from the Deep South who were angered by the president's decision to integrate the armed forces and eliminate discrimination in federal hiring practices and by the decision made following a fiery speech by Minneapolis Mayor Hubert Humphrey at the National Convention in Philadelphia to add a civil rights plank to the Democratic Party Platform.

The Dixiecrats, as they called themselves, backed the candidacy of South Carolina Governor Strom Thurmond.

Also departing were some in the far left wing of the party, who backed the Progressive Party candidate, Henry Wallace, the vice president who had been jilted four years earlier when Roosevelt added Truman to the ticket.

With the Democrats appearing hopelessly split, the Republican candidate, once again New York Governor Thomas Dewey, seemed destined to be the next president.

Dewey adopted a rocking chair approach to campaigning, trying to avoid making mistakes by holding few campaign events, figuring all he had to do was play it safe and he would be elected.

Truman used the same tactics he used from his earliest days running for office in Jackson County- he took his case to the people.

The only way to ensure Truman could as meet as many people as possible was by train. He decided on a well-publicized campaign tour on a special train, the *Ferdinand Magellan*, where he would speak at each stop from the rear platform of the observation car.

Truman explained the reasoning for his whistle stop tour to biographer Merle Miller:

I just got on a train and started across the country to tell people what was going on. I wanted to talk to them face-to-face.

When you get on the television, you're wearing a lot of powder and paint that somebody else put on your face and you haven't even combed your own hair.

But when you're standing right there in front of them and talking to them and shaking their hands if it's possible, the people can tell whether you're telling them the facts or not.

The whistle stop tours covered most of the nation and included a swing through Missouri in late September.

Lamar was not one of the stops. The closest the tour came to Lamar was Neosho about 50 miles away. It also made stops at Monett and Springfield.

Five thousand people greeted Truman when he arrived in Neosho 8 p.m. Wednesday, September 29, about 40 minutes late.

The crowd applauded as a smiling, waving Truman emerged on the platform, accompanied by Bess and Margaret.

"I have spent a lot of time in Neosho," he said, "but then I didn't create so much commotion."

It did not take long for Truman to give the audience what it had been waiting for- a full-throated attack on the Republicans.

"The real issue of this campaign is special privilege against the common people. The good-for-nothing Republican 80th Congress provided this and I am asking you to give me a Democratic Congress so that I can get something done for the people."

As the train pulled out of Neosho, Truman shouted, "I'll come back when I can stay longer."

∞

When the *Chicago Daily Tribune* jumped the gun with its infamous "Dewey defeats Truman" headline and Truman held the newspaper aloft at the St. Louis Union Station, it guaranteed Truman's victory would be recorded in history as one of the great political upsets.

In truth, it was anything but that.

Not only was the election not even close, but the idea that Dewey was an overwhelming favorite to win was created by a number of misconceptions.

Twelve years earlier, a *Literary Digest* poll famously said

Kansas Gov. Alf Landon would defeat Roosevelt by a final margin of 57 percent to 32 percent of the vote and prevent him from earning a second term.

After Roosevelt received just under 61 percent of the vote and received 523 electoral votes to eight for Landon, an examination of the poll showed its fatal flaw- though the magazine took a wide sampling, it consisted of people who subscribed to the magazine, had telephones or owned automobiles. In other words, the people who were surveyed had more money than the average American citizen.

The same flaws existed in 1948, though not quite as pronounced. Not only did the polls still tilt toward the well to do, but they vastly underrepresented minority voters.

Truman's electoral doom was forecast when the Democratic Party split into three segments with some casting their lot with Strom Thurmond and others with Henry Wallace.

The defections actually served to strengthen Truman's hand. When the Dixiecrats bolted because of Truman and the Democratic Party platform's principled stand on civil rights, it greatly increased Truman's support among the black community, something that went unnoticed in the polls.

Surprisingly, the Wallace wing's defection harmed Dewey more than it did Truman. Those joining Wallace's quixotic bid for the presidency, included those who were on the far left wing, including Communist sympathizers, blocking Dewey and the Republicans from making a credible claim that the Democratic Party was the party of communism.

Those factors, combined with Dewey's decision not to take the battle to Truman and the Democrats and Truman's aggressive style of campaigning, in retrospect, make it hard to see how the result could have been different.

When the final vote was recorded, Truman was easily elected with 303 electoral votes to 189 for Dewey, 39 for Thurmond and none for Wallace.

Truman won 28 states and 24,179,347 votes to 16 states and 21,991,292 votes for Dewey and four states and 1,175,930 votes for Thurmond.

Unlike in 1944, when even Truman's vice presidential nomination speech in Lamar was unable to convince Barton County voters to support the Roosevelt-Truman ticket, four years later, the team of Truman and Alben Barkley had no problem capturing the city or county.

In Barton County, Truman received 2,962 votes to 2,554 for Dewey, reversing the result of the 1944 election when Dewey won the county.

Lamar voters chose the Truman-Barkley ticket by a 955-629 margin.

In the pages of the *Lamar Democrat*, Madeleine Aull Van-Hafften seemed practically giddy in her description of Democratic victories nationwide, in Missouri and in Lamar and Barton County.

No longer can the Dixiecrats, the crackpot Wallace forces and the various lunatic fringes point to the Democratic Party as decadent and predict the rise of two, possibly three parties from the ashes of its pyre.

And best of all, it seemed to us, was the vote of confidence and pride extended to the native son by the voters of Barton County and the City of Lamar.

The resurgence of the Democratic Party and the victory

for Harry S. Truman were things Madeleine's father fervently wanted.

Sadly, when the day came, Arthur Aull was not there to celebrate.

CHAPTER THIRTY

Tears were still streaming down Madeleine's cheek as she sat behind her typewriter at the *Democrat* office during the pre-dawn hours and wrote the most difficult story she had ever written.

Arthur Aull, 75, nationally known, widely quoted editor of this paper and father of the writer, is dead.

The death was not unexpected. Aull had been ill for six years and had been confined to his home since February 1947. A week earlier he suffered a severe heart attack and though he rallied for a few days at the beginning of the next week, Aull died Friday, May 7, 1948.

Now, just a few hours later, Madeleine was writing his obituary, which would be published in the Saturday, May 8 *Democrat*. Ironically, the news of the passing of the man who was arguably the second best known man from Lamar was revealed on the same day as the 64th birthday of the first, President Truman.

Madeleine was only following her father's instructions. In the days before his death, Aull insisted the *Democrat* not miss any issues because of his death and that it be published on the day of his funeral.

The biggest story in that day's *Democrat* had to be the death of its most prominent resident. Madeleine was the newspaper's editor and reporter. Therefore, she was the one who tried, unsuccessfully, to set aside her grief and write the story.

This great and understanding soul slipped from its earthly moorings at 11:30 Friday night. And the country editor whose name was known from coast to coast set out upon that uncharted sea where there be no pain.

The article, which ran 70 column inches, detailed his career, described Aull as a "great patriot and civic leader," who was "devoted to the Democratic Party."

Aull's funeral was held Monday, May 10, at Memorial Hall. All businesses were closed at the request of Lamar Mayor Carrol Combs and more than 500 came to pay their respects to a man who had played a prominent role in their lives for nearly a half century.

Aull's friend, Judge John Flanigan from Carthage, delivered the eulogy, which included a reading of Aull's Creed of Life, which he had published in the *Democrat* in 1921, poetry and a tribute to the deceased.

The death of Arthur Aull has cost Lamar its foremost citizen. Journalism has lost one of its brightest stars and truth has lost a loyal friend.

For more than 40 years, Arthur Aull labored with pen and mind and heart for the good of this community.

Flanigan spoke of the national fame Aull received and ended the eulogy by noting the impact Aull and the *Democrat* had on Lamar.

In journalism, his guiding star was truth.

He sought the exact and literal truth no more and no less, believing it to be the chief function of the press to tell the truth without coloring or bias.

Nothing worthy has been attempted or accomplished in Lamar in 40 years that did not have his support.

He loved his town and its people and if sometimes his pen seemed dipped in gall, it was only because of the intensity of his love.

At the conclusion of the service, Nell Casement, who had worked with Aull in the business office of the *Democrat* and handled circulation, directed 12 of the newspaper's young carriers to remove the flowers from the casket. Aull was carried out of Memorial Hall, loaded into a hearse and taken to his final resting place at Lake Cemetery.

Luanna Aull and her three daughters received condolences from across the nation, including a message from Lamar's most prominent native son.

The telegram came from the White House through President Truman's press secretary Charles G. Ross:

The president was greatly distressed to hear of the death of Mr. Arthur Aull, widely known editor of the Lamar Democrat. An able and picturesque figure in American journalism has passed on.

After several days passed, a subtle change of one word was made on the masthead of the *Lamar Democrat*.

No longer did it read "*Lamar Democrat* published by Ar-

Luanna Aull. *Photo courtesy of the Barton County Historical Society*

thur Aull."

Now it read *"Lamar Democrat* published by Mrs. Arthur Aull."

Madeleine was determined that the newspaper also remain as close as possible to the way her father had written and published it.

And for a while, that formula proved successful.

Less than two weeks after Truman's resounding election victory, Lamar received an unwelcome reminder of one of the most tragic episodes in the city's history when two of the three men sentenced to life in prison for their roles in the murders of Barton County Sheriff Roy Patterson and his son Sammie escaped.

The Huston brothers, George and Ernest, who were serving their sentences in the state penitentiary in Jefferson City, were given permission to attend the funeral of their mother, Gertrude Huston, in Excelsior Springs November 14.

Two Highway Patrol troopers escorted them. The Hustons were allowed to go into their mother's house to meet with the assorted relatives and friends who were gathered there.

Whether they took the time to reacquaint themselves is not certain because it did not take long for the troopers to be told by one of those inside that the Huston brothers had slipped out through a back door, something which angered their relatives who felt they were disrespecting their mother's memory.

Despite the interruption of the solemn occasion, the funeral continued as planned.

While no one expected them to come anywhere near Lamar, the news was still upsetting for those who loved the Pattersons.

Both men were captured within eight days.

Ernest was arrested in Richmond, Missouri, at the home of Myrtle Rush, the mother of Monroe Rush, who had confessed to shooting the Pattersons. His plan was for Rush to hide him. She did not agree with the plan and called the police.

George Huston was located in a barn 18 miles northeast of Richmond wrapped in a blanket under a pile of hay.

CHAPTER THIRTY-ONE

As the time approached for Harry Truman's inauguration, excitement grew after it was learned that Lamar would be represented in the inaugural parade.

The city where Truman was born in 1884, the son of a simple mule trader and his wife, would be represented by a wagon drawn by a team of Missouri mules, two of them owned by Claude "Brother" Adams, who raised mules at a location at the southeast corner of the intersection of highways 160 and 71 just west of Lamar and the other two owned by Ed Knell of Carthage.

Adams, 43, who had been raising mules since 1914 when he was nine years old, was justly proud of his mules and word of Lamar's representation in the inaugural parade was spread quickly due to coverage from regional newspapers and wire services and locally through the *Democrat*.

"Every one of my mules has won a blue ribbon somewhere," Adams told a reporter. "They're fine mules. We like to think we're breeding as good a mule as you'll find anywhere in Missouri."

Besides John Anderson Truman and his son's connection

to mules, the animals had a long and storied history in the state.

The legend of the Missouri mules began in 1840 when the animals were brought in from Mexico by the Santa Fe Trail to help farmers work the fields.

Mules were a product of the mating of a male donkey and a mare and Brother Adams' mules were no ordinary specimens.

The animals Adams and Knell were taking to Washington, D. C. were created by breeding the jacks with Belgian mares.

Claude "Brother" Adams of Lamar drove a wagon pulled by his mules along Pennsylvania Avenue as part of the Truman inaugural parade in January 1949. *Photo courtesy of Truman Library and Museum*

The four sleek blond sorrel 1,200 pound mules- Blondie and Duke owned by Adams and Beck and Polly owned by Knell- were distinguished by their flowing white manes, tails and undersides.

Though initially there was talk of taking the mules to Washington, D. C. by train, those plans fell through and Blondie, Duke, Beck and Polly were loaded into a stock truck.

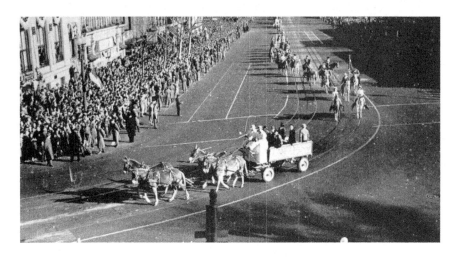

Brother Adams' mules, along with Ed Knell's mules, represented Lamar in the 1949 Inaugural Parade. *Photo courtesy of Truman Library and Museum*

Brother's brother, Billee Bob Adams, was in charge of getting the contingent, which in addition to himself consisted of Knell, Brother, Brother's wife Hazel and their five-year-old son Claude Oscar to the nation's capital.

B. B., 28, began driving a truck at age 14, working with Brother and hauling coal from the coal veins in the small Barton County community of Milford.

After serving in the U. S. Navy during World War II, Adams bought two trucks and a combine and accompanied by his wife Hazel and daughters Tina and Frances followed the wheat harvest through several states before returning to Lamar in 1947, where he operated a trucking business.

Now Billee Bob Adams was entrusted to deliver four Missouri mules to the nation's capital to help inaugurate the son of a Lamar mule trader.

∞

The November 1948 election not only returned to Truman to office, but also gave him, for the first time, Democratic majorities.

That, however, was no guarantee of success as the president discovered January 18, 1949, two days before the inauguration when the Senate voted on a proposal that had already passed the House and was considered to be a formality.

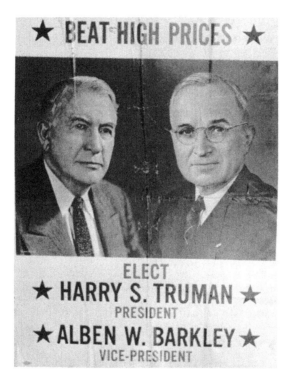

1948 poster for the Truman-Barkley ticket.
Photo courtesy of Truman Library and Museum

Every four years, Congress voted to exempt tickets for the parade grandstands, the inaugural ball and the gala concert from the federal admissions tax.

The Inaugural Committee had already sold out the tickets

for the event and had not charged the tax, even declaring on the tickets that they were tax exempt.

The bill breezed through the House, but ran into a buzz saw in the Senate, where six Democrats joined the Republicans to defeat the bill 47-45, forcing the Inaugural Committee to pay approximately $50,000 in taxes.

Once again, it was Truman's stands in favor of civil rights that created opposition from within his own party.

Voting against the tax exemption were senators Harry Byrd of Virginia, who had once been a member of the Ku Klux Klan, Virgil Chapman of Kentucky, John L. McClellan of Arkansas, Richard E. Russell of Georgia, Edwin Johnson of Colorado and Willis Robertson, father of television evangelist-to-be Pat Robertson, of Virginia.

The Senate also gave Truman a victory, approving his appointment of Dean Acheson as secretary of state by an 83-6 margin.

Acheson would replace George Marshall, whose resignation took effect on January 20.

On the same day, the guests who were staying in Blair House awaiting the inauguration, the president's brother Vivian, his sister Mary Jane and Bess Truman's brothers Frank, George and Frederick Wallace and their wives, went to the White House to watch Margaret play host to a national radio broadcast of a program to raise money for the March of Dimes to help combat childhood polio.

Margaret introduced celebrities who made their pitches to the American people to support the cause including Sen. Margaret Chase Smith of Maine, the first woman elected to the U. S. Senate, novelist Betty Smith, author of *A Tree Grows in Brooklyn*, and former child actress Shirley Temple and her

Sen. Tom Connelly of Texas, Harry Truman and Margaret Truman. *Photo courtesy of Truman Library and Museum*

husband, actor John Agar.

On the same evening, President Truman made an impromptu speech at a pre-inaugural dinner in front of a group of Democrats.

After introducing Bess and vice president-elect Alben Barkley, and making a few after-dinner remarks, the president's speech took a serious turn.

We are faced with a serious situation. No one, I think, in the history of the country assumed a greater responsibility than I did on the 12th day of April at 7:09 in the afternoon when I was sworn in after the death of our great president Franklin Roosevelt.

It was necessary for me at that time to assume an almost unbearable burden. I was willing to assume it because that was my duty. I did the best I could with it over the period from April 12, 1945 until the present day.

Now, Senator Barkley and I have a tremendous responsibility-the greatest burden, I think, that any president and vice president of the United States ever had in the history of our country.

We are going to assume that burden and we are going to do our best to carry out the things that are necessary to meet the situation with which we are faced in this country and in the world.

But we can't do that unless you and the Congress and the people of these United States get behind us and help us carry out those principles that are necessary to get the thing done, to get the peace in this world that we need and that we are going to have.

President Truman had a full day in front of him when he awoke in the pre-dawn hours of Thursday, January 20, 1949, having slept less than five hours.

Temperatures in the low 30s and a brisk wind whipping through the air greeted him as he left the White House for the first event of Inauguration Day, one he eagerly anticipated.

Truman was driven to the Mayflower Hotel, where he had breakfast with his World War I comrades of Battery D, 129th Field Artillery.

As the time neared for the inaugural parade, throngs of people, an estimated one million, lined the parade route on the streets surrounding Pennsylvania Avenue.

In addition to those who were in the nation's capital for the event, millions more would listen to it via broadcasts by the national networks.

The listening audience was not limited to those in the United States. Voice of America reporters were stationed on the Capitol steps and along the parade route and the event would

Missouri's float in the 1949 Inaugural Parade. *Photo courtesy of Truman Library and Museum*

be broadcast throughout the world in 17 languages, thanks to relays through the American base at Munich and the British Broadcasting Corporation.

For the first time since William Howard Taft's wife began the tradition of the First Lady sitting beside the president or president-elect in the first car in the parade, Bess Truman would not be in the car with her husband.

Sen. Barkley joined Truman in the lead car, with Bess seated with Margaret and Barkley's daughter, Marian Barkley Truitt, in the second car.

The swearing-in ceremony began at 12:29 p.m., 29 minutes later than scheduled with the Marine Band playing "Hail to the Chief."

Tens of thousands watched inaugural ceremonies on January 20, 1949.
Photo courtesy of Truman Library and Museum

Associate Supreme Court Justice Stanley Reed swore in Barkley as vice president, then Truman held his right hand aloft and put his left hand on a Bible that was held by Charles E. Cropley, a Supreme Court clerk, and took the oath of office.

In his inaugural speech, the president outlined a vision for America that set a course that has been followed since that time.

I accept with humility the honor which the American people have conferred upon me. I accept it with a deep resolve to do all that I can for the welfare of this nation and for the peace of the world.

In performing the duties of my office, I need the help and prayers of every one of you. I ask for your encouragement and for your support. The tasks we face are difficult and we can accomplish them only if we work together.

Each period of our national history has had its special challenges. Those that confront us now are momentous as any in the past.

Today marks the beginning not only of a new administration, but of a period that will be eventful, perhaps decisive, for us and for the world.

It may be our lot to experience, and in a large measure to bring about, a major turning point in the long history of the human race.

The first half of this century has been marked by unprecedented and brutal attacks on the rights of man and by the two most frightful wars in history.

The supreme need of our time is for men to learn to live together in peace and harmony.

At that point, Truman sent a message not just to the people of the United States, but to the people of the world who were listening through Voice of America that the U. S. would defend their right to freedom and the freedom of the people.

We believe that all men have a right to equal justice under law and equal opportunity to share in the common good.

We believe that all men have the right to freedom of thought and expression. We believe that all men are created equal because they are created in the image of God.

From this faith, we will not be moved.

Truman voiced "vigorous support" for the fledgling United Nations and extolled the virtues of the Marshall Plan through which the U. S. helped in the rebuilding of war-torn Europe.

Our efforts have brought new hope to all mankind. We have beaten back despair and defeatism. We have saved a number of countries from losing their liberty.

Hundreds of millions of people all over the world now agree with us that we need not have war, that we can have peace.

The initiative is ours.

Truman outlined four major courses of action that would be taken to reach the goal.

The first was a continued support of the United Nations,

with the second being a continuation of programs for world economic recovery.

Truman's third course of action was the formation of the framework that became the North Atlantic Treaty Organization (NATO).

We will strengthen freedom-loving nations against the dangers of aggression. We are working out with a number of countries a joint agreement designed to strengthen the security of the North Atlantic area.

Such an agreement would take the form of a collective defense arrangement within the terms of the United Nations Charter.

The fourth course of action called for a new program in which the United States would make the benefits of its scientific advances and industrial progress available to help underdeveloped areas of the world.

The inaugural parade lasted three hours, with Gen. Omar Bradley, Chief of Staff of the Army, serving as grand marshal.

Cadets from West Point, Annapolis and the Coast Guard Academy represented the armed forces in the parade, while each state had various bands and marching units.

A highlight of the parade was the appearance of Brother Adams and Ed Knell's sorrel mules Blondie, Duke, Beck and Polly.

Adams and Knell, dressed in white overalls, drove the team down Pennsylvania Avenue hitched to a light spring rubber-tired wagon with the words "Lamar, Missouri, the birthplace of President Harry S. Truman," written in bold, prominent letters on the side.

The mules were champions most of the route, but shied at one point before Adams and Knell were able to get them under control.

Adams blamed the near mishap on a boy on roller skates.

When the parade was over and Brother Adams was on his way back to Lamar, he offered the highest praise he could give a president to Harry Truman.

"He seems to know a lot about mules."

President Truman with a Missouri mule following the inaugural parade on January 20, 1949. *Photo courtesy of Truman Library and Museum*

CHAPTER THIRTY-TWO

As the end of 1949 was approaching, nearly a year and half had passed since the death of Arthur Aull and the *Lamar Democrat* was still unmistakably his newspaper.

While that was the *Democrat's* greatest strength, it was also its greatest weakness.

Madeleine continued to operate the newspaper in exactly the same way as her father had.

She began her day making the same rounds Aull had used when gathering the news for the afternoon paper. She covered the courthouse news with the same spare-no-details philosophy that made the newspaper so distinctive.

Just like her father, when people wrote negative letters to the editor, lambasting the *Democrat* for printing information the writer felt should never have been made public or claimed that an article was inaccurate, the letter was printed prominently, often on page one, and in its entirety.

The approach was the same and Madeleine, like her father, had a way with words, but she was not Arthur Aull.

With Aull gone, the readers from across the country who had continued their subscriptions year after year to read about the latest shenanigans of the people of Lamar and Barton County gradually began to let their subscriptions expire.

The *Democrat's* out-of-town subscribers, like those of most newspapers, were now almost entirely people who had some connection to Lamar.

Madeleine was able to duplicate her father's blow-by-blow descriptions of divorces, but she lacked the light touch Arthur Aull often applied to his work.

Madeleine also ran headlong into people's expectations of that time that reporting, especially the bare knuckles brand of reporting that the Aulls practiced, was a man's game.

Women were usually relegated to writing social news and recipes.

Arthur Aull not only had the advantages of being the right gender for the time, but he had a distinguished scholarly look to him that commanded respect.

Along with the rampant sexism of the time, many judged Madeleine by her appearance. Her wardrobe invariably consisted of long dark-colored dresses and her hair pulled up severely in a bun.

To that ensemble, she invariably added one of her collection of colorful hats.

When people entered the *Democrat* office on the north side of the square, Madeleine's desk was one of the first things they saw.

They were also greeted by the slight haze caused by Madeleine's chain smoking habit.

She was not what people expected.

Madeleine was not the stern presence at the *Democrat* that her outward appearance or her writing might indicate she would be.

Though her language could sometimes be rough, she was not feared among her co-workers.

"I had the greatest respect for Madeleine," said Dorothy Parks, who was a typesetter at the *Democrat*.

"People always made fun of her, this weird little woman with the hat on and she always had a serious look on her face, but she always worked hard."

Her journalism philosophy remained the exact same as her father's as she continued his life's work and never altered her approach.

"She headed out the door in the morning with a pad and pencil," Parks said, "and she would come back in about 11 a.m. and start writing and by three or four o'clock she would have everything back to us."

Madeleine continued to follow her father's teachings without any variance, where Aull never hesitated to call a scoundrel a scoundrel, neither did his daughter.

Both of them, however, had one type of person who was never criticized.

"I went in one day when she was typing up someone's obituary. She was just moaning and groaning," Parks recalled. "I said, 'Madeleine, what's wrong? What's the matter?'

" 'Well, Dorothy, my dad always told me you can't call a dead man a son of a bitch.' She wanted to call him an SOB, but she couldn't do it. She had to find some nicer things to write about him."

One area in which Madeleine could not replicate her father's success was on the business end of the newspaper. Neither she nor Nell Casement, who had worked a quarter of a century on the business and circulation end of the newspaper, were anywhere nearly as adept as Arthur Aull.

Fortunately, the only competition was the *Lamar Republican*, which appeared to be in danger of closing at any time.

As long as no serious challenger to the *Democrat* existed, it managed to continue to be profitable, though less so than before Aull's death.

That started changing in late 1949 when the *Republican* sold to Dewey Wayne Rowland, 26, a recent graduate of the University of Missouri School of Journalism.

D. Wayne Rowland was a veteran, having served in the U. S. Army in Europe during World War II as a first lieutenant in field artillery.

Rowland also had experience in newspapers, starting as a police reporter for the *Columbia Tribune* and then buying a couple of small town weeklies in Willow Springs and Seymour.

Rowland bought the failing *Lamar Republican* and changed the name of the publication to the *Lamar Journal*. He wanted no public perception of affiliation with any political party.

The newspaper office was relocated to a newer two-story building a block north of the square. The second story was remodeled to serve as a home for Rowland, his wife Maxine and their children and a recent Seymour High School graduate named Irene Smith, who served as a combination nanny and assistant for the Rowlands.

Rowland began changing the look of the *Journal*, updating it to where it looked more like a 1950s publication rather than a relic of the 1920s and developed a plan to cut into the stranglehold the Aull family had on the Lamar newspaper business.

It was not long before he was joined in that venture by someone with the talent and drive to make things even more difficult for Madeleine Aull VanHafften.

Shortly after Rowland moved to Lamar, another newcomer

made his way to the city, one destined to have an even more lasting impact on the city.

When he returned from his three-year tour of duty in the Aleutians, Gerald Gilkey used the money he had saved and bought an auto parts business. After a couple of years, with the store not doing well and he and Betty having an infant son Steve, he sold the business and went to work for his brothers-in-law, Jewell and Gerald Medlin, at an Oldsmobile dealership in Fort Scott, Kansas.

On the first day at his new job Gilkey, a natural salesman, sold one of the highest priced cars Oldsmobile made, an Olds 98.

With business going well, the Medlin brothers decided they wanted to move closer to home and in 1950 opened an Oldsmobile dealership in Lamar.

As the Medlins made arrangements to open the Lamar dealership, Gilkey remain in Fort Scott, charged with selling as many of the remaining 14 cars on the lot as possible.

Gilkey bought a full-page newspaper advertisement and radio time and within eight days all 14 cars had been sold and he was on his way to a new life in Lamar.

After his marriage to Ione Williams in 1945, Richard Chancellor had to find to place for himself in the home he had left behind to fight for his country.

By this time, H. C. Chancellor, well into his 70s, was turning more of the day-to-day duties of running the Travelers Hotel over to his oldest son Harold, though he continued to play an active role in the hotel's management.

Harold brought his younger brother into the business, but the fit was not a satisfying one. Richard Chancellor had been an Army Air Force officer, a leader of men and even though the money came in handy, he wanted more.

It was not long before he opened a hardware store on the square and it was an almost immediate success, but the hardware business did not provide the type of challenge Chancellor wanted.

As he and Ione began raising a family, Chancellor wanted more than a retail business could provide.

As the calendar turned from the 1940s to the 1950s, Chancellor, now 32, had to face the problem faced by so many veterans returning from the war.

During the war, he developed a skill set and talents that suited him well in the military, but how could he use those talents in a way that would enable him to take care of his family and allow him to make a difference in his community?

CHAPTER THIRTY-THREE

When Marvin VanGilder's father moved the family from Lamar to Stockton at the end of 1941, VanGilder, who had been working as a high school reporter and printer's devil at the *Lamar Republican*, found no outlets for his writing.

Thankfully, it was not long before J. T. VanGilder's employer, the Sac-Osage Electric Cooperative, placed its permanent headquarters in another Cedar County town, El Dorado Springs.

VanGilder, a high school junior, wrote movie reviews for the *El Dorado Springs Sun* and spent two years serving as editor of the *El-Hi-Mo,* El Dorado Springs High School's weekly newspaper.

After graduating in 1944, VanGilder attended Drury College in Springfield where he was a feature writer for the campus newspaper, the *Mirror*, and worked part-time as a stringer for Springfield Newspapers and KGBX Radio.

VanGilder's first full-time job after graduating from Drury in 1948 was as a teacher in the Mansfield, Missouri school, but he continued to pursue his writing to supplement the meager salary he received as a public school teacher, with free-lance

Marvin VanGilder (center) with two fellow Jasper School faculty members in 1949. *Photo provided by Marvin VanGilder to Lamar Press*

reporting for newspapers in Springfield, Mansfield, Marshfield and Seymour.

It was at Seymour that VanGilder first came into contact with D. Wayne Rowland.

After one year at Mansfield, VanGilder returned to the area where he spent his formative years.

"When I moved back to 'God's Country' to become music supervisor in the Jasper public schools, I found that same man (Rowland) had just purchased the *Lamar Republican*, my original launching pad," VanGilder wrote.

While VanGilder did not immediately begin working for the rechristened *Lamar Journal*, he immediately reaped benefits from Rowland's move to Lamar.

VanGilder found himself attracted to Irene Smith, the young woman who served as an assistant and nanny for the Rowlands.

"She and I had encountered each other on two previous occasions," VanGilder wrote, remembering those instances many years later, "but it was not until a friend introduced us at Lamar and I made a date to visit her at the Rowland office/ residence that the inevitable spark was ignited."

In October 1950, Marvin L. VanGilder and Irene Smith exchanged vows at the bride's church in Seymour. The couple moved to Seymour where VanGilder had taken a position in the public school system.

From afar, VanGilder maintained interest in the battle for Lamar newspaper supremacy.

Though he never publicly expressed any contempt at the type of newspaper the Aulls published, his description of Rowland's *Lamar Journal* product made it clear what he thought of the *Lamar Democrat*.

The Journal was a polished, professionally designed daily publication with attractive typefaces and varied type sizes for headlines and photo captions, modern vocabulary, objective editorial policies, a strong bent for community promotion and a positive outlook, quality writing and design style and frequent illustrations.

It was in fact the first Lamar newspaper that could boast most of those characteristics.

Lamar readers noticed.

With a viable alternative to the Aull style of journalism, the *Democrat* continued to have solid circulation in Lamar and Barton County, but advertising revenue fell.

Luanna Aull and Madeleine feared that the newspaper could not survive at this rate.

And the *Journal* was showing no signs of fading.

D. Wayne Rowland's determination that his newspaper play a neutral role in political matters and offer an objective viewpoint did not change Madeleine's approach or her unabashed support for the Democratic Party.

That support was especially strong for President Truman.

Arthur Aull, after initially expressing distaste for Truman's connection to the crooked Pendergast machine, became a staunch supporter of the president and Madeleine shared that sentiment.

When Truman was embroiled in controversy, as he was after he fired General Douglas MacArthur in April 1951, a move that proved to be unpopular with the nation at large given the general's reputation, Madeleine leaped to the president's defense.

When the hullabaloo raised by the Republicans for strictly political purposes has somewhat subsided and the hero worshippers have run the gamut of emotion, it is highly probable that the people on the whole will agree that President Truman could do nothing other than to relieve General McArthur (sic) of the Far

Eastern command.

The firing of MacArthur took place after the general had not only disagreed with Truman's conduct of the Korean Conflict, but had made foreign policy pronouncements that were in direct contrast to the official U. S. foreign policy as directed by Truman.

In his memoirs, Truman, always a voracious reader of history, compared the situation he faced with that faced by Abraham Lincoln when General McClellan, another military leader with political ambitions, had caused him similar problems.

Lincoln was patient, for that was his nature, but at long last he was compelled to relieve the Union Army's principal commander. And though I gave the difficulty with MacArthur much wearisome thought, I realized that I would have no other choice myself than to relieve the nation's top field commander.

If there is one basic element in our Constitution, it is civilian control of the military. Politics are to be made by the elected political officials, not by generals or admirals.

Truman weighed the decision, was provoked by MacArthur again when he learned the general had criticized him to members of Congress and realized the situation was untenable.

On April 11, 1951, the following statement was released:

With deep regret, I have concluded that General of the Army Douglas MacArthur is unable to give his wholehearted support to the policies of the United States Government and of the United Nations in matters pertaining to his official duties.

In view of the specific responsibilities imposed upon me by the Constitution of the United States and the added responsibility which has been entrusted to me by the United Nations, I have decided I must make a change of command in the Far East.

I have therefore relieved General MacArthur of his commands and have designated Lieutenant General Matthew B. Ridgway as his successor.

Truman's decision created an uproar and his political opponents began talk of having him removed from office.

Madeleine and the *Lamar Democrat* were having none of it.

Of all the histrionics that have been indulged in by the enemies of the president, the foolish mention of impeachment seems to us the epitome of lack of understanding of the meaning of the world and general childishness.

There weren't enough people who shared Madeleine's way of thinking and polls showed Truman's popularity dipping to barely more than 20 percent.

Facing that grim reality, Truman, the last person who could have served more than two terms as president after the states ratified the 22nd Amendment, decided it was time to go home to Missouri and did not seek re-election.

When January 1953 arrived and Dwight D. Eisenhower replaced Truman as commander in chief, Lamar became the birthplace of a former president.

In 1953, for the first time, Lamar residents would be able to dial for long distance calls, instead of having the calls placed by an operator.

Loyd Gathman, serving his first year as mayor after more than a decade on the City Council, was given the honor of making the first call and that call went to President Truman.

"I apologized to him for calling," Gathman recalled, "and we had an ordinary conversation. He said it was nice of me to call and he was very grateful."

CHAPTER THIRTY-FOUR

In the fall of 1929, Betty Aull, the youngest daughter of Arthur Aull, met the man with whom she wanted to spend the rest of her life.

At the time, Betty was in her first and only year at the University of Missouri School of Journalism in Columbia after deciding to change her major and specialize in advertising.

She was introduced to Stan White, a fellow advertising major and the journalism school's student body president.

"It was the romance of the campus," she recalled 60 years later. After a suitable courtship, they sealed their engagement by following an old tradition.

"There was a bridge that ran over a small stream and that's where journalism students would go when they fell in love to seal their engagement.

"We went there and had our engagement kiss."

The engagement period lasted far longer than either of them wanted.

After they graduated, Stan took a job in St. Louis to earn money while Betty returned to Lamar and sold advertising for her father.

Their wedding was further delayed in January 1932 when Betty nearly lost her life in a tragic accident in which the car she was riding in was broadsided by a milk truck. The driver, a friend, was killed and it took a year and a half for Betty to recover.

Stan White and Betty Aull were married February 23, 1934 in Springfield. The couple moved several times over the next couple of decades as White took advertising jobs in newspapers and radio, interrupted by four years of active duty in the U. S. Navy during World War II, where he was a lieutenant commander in charge of a destroyer escort.

In 1953, White changed jobs once more, this time deliberately taking a pay cut.

Luanna Aull made the announcement in the September 29, 1953 *Democrat*:

It has been my sincere desire and the desire of my late husband, Arthur Aull, that the paper remain in the hands of the Aull family. My daughter, Madeleine, has done a fine job in carrying the torch laid down by her father.

But as the town has grown and the potential of the paper increased, she has become increasingly aware of the fact that she stands in need of loyal assistance, particularly in the field of advertising, for which she has little taste and less professional training.

We both are therefore happy to announce that my son-in-law Stanley E. White has agreed to come to Lamar to provide this assistance.

Madeleine will occupy her present position as editor, setting the policy of the paper and handling all of the news. Stan will become the advertising manager. As to the handling of the business and mechanics in connection with the operation, the two will function on a partnership basis.

Stan White assumed his new duties with only one previous daily newspaper advertising position, but it made him uniquely qualified for the challenge that awaited him.

He had rescued the newspaper in the hometown of a future president (though he never knew it) when he was advertising manager in Hope, Arkansas.

Had he arrived in time to save a newspaper in the hometown of a former president?

The *Lamar Journal* was on a roll when Stan and Betty White arrived.

While the *Democrat* ran almost no photos, the Leader featured them in every issue. The *Democrat* ran crime and courtroom scandals while the *Journal* focused relentlessly on a positive product designed to make readers feel better about the world when they finished reading it.

And the *Journal* had the youth, energy and many talents of Marvin VanGilder.

VanGilder, still shy of his 30th birthday, left his teaching job in Seymour to take a position teaching music in the Golden City School District 17 miles east of Lamar.

During the summer months, VanGilder worked full-time at the *Journal,* writing feature articles, something that had never been seen in Lamar newspapers, offering coverage of the arts, especially music and provided coverage of the communities surrounding Lamar, ranging from Mindenmines and Liberal near the Missouri-Kansas line to Lockwood in Dade County, a town that was approximately 25 miles east of Lamar.

The most popular articles VanGilder contributed to the *Jour-*

nal were the regular columns he wrote on the history of Lamar and Barton County.

VanGilder turned out a tremendous volume of copy and all written in his unique eloquent style.

In the summer, he even sold subscriptions and was quite adept at doing so.

During the school year, he still wrote a considerable amount.

He did all of this while serving as a lay preacher at area churches.

VanGilder also took an active role in the community, most noticeably in his role championing the formation of the Barton County Historical Society. Though he had a marked preference for the Republican Party, VanGilder contacted a prominent Democrat and received the following response:

In reply to yours of July 23, I think it is a grand thing for you to organize a Barton County Historical Society. It will be a wonderful thing for you to work in cooperation with the State Historical Society and I know you can make a contribution that will be well worthwhile.

I was born in Lamar on May 8, 1884, but left there for Cass and Jackson counties when I was about a year old and was not able to get back to Lamar again until the senatorial campaign of 1934. I have always thought very highly of Lamar.

Sincerely yours,

Harry S Truman

With all of his interests and little spare time, VanGilder also had another project that he hoped would have a lasting benefit for the people of Barton County.

VanGilder was working diligently to write a comprehensive history of Barton County to be published in 1955 in connection with the county's centennial celebration.

OO

The outlook was brighter for the *Lamar Democrat* after the arrival of Stan and Betty White.

Though the look of the newspaper remained much the same, it truly was a family affair with Betty writing social items and working in the office and Stan selling advertising and writing sports, an area that had been sorely neglected.

The newspaper began printing more school news.

Madeleine continued to do what Madeleine had always done and what her father had done for 46 years before his illness forced him to retire.

Despite the addition of two more people to the payroll, the *Democrat's* financial picture improved almost immediately.

It wasn't just the added advertising sales. Stan White's presence lightened a building that had never quite escaped the sadness of Arthur Aull's departure. There was little doubt that he was running the business and that lightened the load for Madeleine and left her to do the work she enjoyed the most.

Dorothy Parks, who worked at the *Democrat* in later years, described what White meant to the newspaper.

"He was real enjoyable to work for. I had a great deal of respect for him. He was real considerate of all of us.

"He was always the same, always easygoing."

Another former *Democrat* employee, Opal Young, in a 1989 interview, said, "He always expected the most from his staff and seemed confident he was going to get it. He had a way of making each of us feel special and needed."

Ten months after Stan and Betty White arrived, the competition ended when the *Democrat* bought the *Journal* and shut it down.

If both papers had continued, it was not certain which would have prevailed, but as the competition increased, *Journal* Publisher D. Wayne Rowland decided it was time to leave the newspaper business and seek a career in academics, a career that would eventually lead to him becoming chairman of the news department at the University of Syracuse, dean of the Drake University School of Journalism and founder of a communications school in the Philippines before his death at age 66 in 1989.

He remained an influence on southwest Missouri journalism for decades after his 1954 departure.

"His influence upon the Lamar business community was a positive and progressive one that inspired a healthy degree of boldness in advertising and promotion," Marvin VanGilder wrote.

While Rowland's journalistic practices had an influence, his primary impact came in the encouragement he offered to one of his employees.

"Wayne Rowland was a personal friend who helped turn my attention toward journalism as a full-time central career," VanGilder wrote.

The demise of the *Journal* left VanGilder in a difficult position as far as his history of Barton County was concerned. For the next several months, when he had time he sold advertising for the publication to make it possible.

Finally, on July 23, 1955, he sent the following letter to those who had purchased advertising:

Advertising response has not been sufficient to make it possible for us to print The Story of Barton County at this time. Therefore, the amount which you contributed for this purpose is being returned.

I am very sorry we are unable to complete this project, as I feel it would have been of immeasurable value to the people of the county for generations to come.

Your contribution indicates that you agree with this point of view. However, many others do not.

Nevertheless, I am determined that The Story of Barton County shall be printed and made available to the people of the county, eventually, in some form. When this happens, you will be given proper credit for your support.

I have neither sought nor expected financial gain from this project. The story is written and I will gladly make available the information it contains to anyone who has need of it. I continue to believe that ours is a history worth remembering, one of which we may be forever proud.

Thanks again for your support.

Marvin L. VanGilder

VanGilder resigned from his teaching position at Golden City and began working full-time in journalism at the *Carthage Evening Press.*

He was leaving the teaching profession behind, but he never abandoned his plan to publish a history of an area he loved.

CHAPTER THIRTY-FIVE

The big sign in front of the house greeted visitors, "Harry S Truman, President of the United States was born here- Everett Earp Owner."

Fewer people were visiting Truman's birthplace since Eisenhower became president. No marketing campaign existed to promote the house where a president had been born.

"My pappy bought this place from the Truman family," Earp said.

That wasn't true. John and Martha Truman had been gone for more than 35 years when Earp's father bought the house.

As Earp guided a visitor through the house, he came to the room where the future president had been 71 years earlier. "On a bed like this, in this here spot, is where Harry Truman was born.

"My pappy saw him when he was a mighty puny baby only eight hours old."

The truth of that story was debatable, but it was a good story.

On the wall and not quite fitting in with the Truman concept was an article on Wyatt Earp. "Wyatt was my cousin.

I've been a two-gun sheriff. My boy's a two-gun sheriff in California.

"When those Puerto Rican desperadoes started shooting at Harry that time in Washington," Earp said, referring to an assassination attempt against Truman, "me and my boy said, "What Harry needs is us."

Fortunately, Truman was unharmed during that attempt despite not having the Earps with him.

Earp's health was declining and he confided in the visitor.

"I hope Lamar keeps (this house) as a museum when I'm gone."

During the first week of November 1956, Everett Earp suffered a stroke. He died November 8 at the age of 74 in the house where Harry Truman was born.

During the early part of 1948, Earp had been in touch with state officials about the possibility of selling the home. A state appraisal showed the house to be worth $750, just $65 more than John Truman paid for it in 1882.

State officials were willing to go above that figure, with the backing of the legislature all the way to $15,000, to buy the house, but not for Earp's $30,000 asking price.

When Earp saw he was not going to get what he hoped for, he brought the price down to $25,000, but that was still far more than state officials were willing to pay.

Earp died eight years later still the owner of Truman's birthplace.

Officials in the Kansas City and St. Louis locals of United Auto Workers heard reports that the house was slowly deteriorating and stepped in. The union was appreciative of the contributions Truman had made to the cause of organized labor and on April 30, 1957, the national UAW paid $6,000 to buy the former president's birthplace from the Earp family with the intention of restoring it to the way it looked on May 8, 1884 and presenting it to the state of Missouri to become a shrine for Truman.

A porch that had been added to the house in later years and all remnants of the approximately 35 years the Earps owned the house were removed.

Those involved in the restoration process had no way of knowing what happened to the original furniture, but carefully researched the time and added appropriate period furniture.

Fresh coats of paint were applied to the structure and a large granite monument was placed on the grounds with the inscription offering highlights of Truman's political career.

With the UAW's painstaking restoration of the building, done in cooperation with the Missouri State Parks Department, completed, all that remained was to hold an official ceremony turning the building over to the state and to the people of Missouri.

Initially, there was thought of holding the ceremony on May 8, 1959, Truman's 75th birthday, but the Democratic National Committee had arranged a fundraising activity for that day with a national radio and television broadcast centered on Truman's birthday, so after making sure Truman would be able to make it, the dedication of the Truman Birthplace was scheduled for Sunday, April 19, 1959.

Not only was there great anticipation in the city for Truman's first visit in nearly 15 years, but the event would also include two politicians widely expected to be contenders for the Democratic presidential nomination in 1960, Sen. Stuart Symington, who had agreed to deliver the address at the dedication and the Senate Majority Leader Lyndon B. Johnson of

Texas. At the last minute, Johnson was unable to attend due to other commitments.

In the *Democrat*, Madeleine reported on the rumor that was circulating in Missouri political circles.

The dedication, some political observers were inclined to believe, might serve as a strategic time and place for an announcement by the former president publicly favoring the candidacy of Missouri's Senator Symington for the Democratic presidential nomination.

Truman's return promised to be the biggest event in Lamar since his 1944 visit.

∞

During the 1950s, Gerald Gilkey continued selling Oldsmobiles for the Medlin brothers and became a well-known and well-liked member of the Lamar community.

As the decade neared an end, he was certain that he wanted to own a car dealership. The only thing that stood in his way was the knowledge that in order to do so, he and Betty would have to leave Lamar.

Gilkey did not intend to compete with his wife's family by buying a competitor in Lamar.

In 1959, another opportunity of a different kind presented itself.

Stan White, who by this time served as a co-publisher of the *Democrat*, approached Gilkey about running for City Council. White appreciated Gilkey's work ethic, his ability to get along with people and his honesty.

After giving it much consideration and consulting with Betty, Gilkey put his name into consideration and received the nomination of the Lamar Democratic Party during its caucus in the Barton County Courthouse.

The Ward One council seat was being vacated by Norbert Heim, the Democratic nominee for mayor, who was already assured of election because the city's Republicans, at their caucus, which was also held at the courthouse, agreed to nominate the much-respected Heim despite his Democratic Party affiliation.

Gilkey was elected to the Lamar City Council in April as one of two Ward One representatives.

During the same election, Richard Chancellor was elected to a second term as Ward Two councilman.

Chancellor had sold his hardware business on the square years earlier and had taken an upper management position with Lamar's biggest employer, the Lawn Boy manufacturing plant, a position in which he was once again able to utilize the leadership abilities he had honed during the years in the Army Air Force.

Mayor Loyd Gathman was determined that Lamar put its best foot forward when Harry Truman and the national media returned to the city for the dedication of the Truman Birthplace.

It was not the first time he had been involved with the planning for a visit by Truman. Gathman was serving on the City Council on August 31, 1944 when Truman accepted the vice presidential nomination.

Gathman issued a notice encouraging city residents to make sure their lawns were "neatly clipped and flowers dis-

Continued on Page 2, Column 6

Lamar made the top of page one on the April 20, 1959 New York Times, just as it did on September 1, 1944, following Truman's vice presidential nomination acceptance speech.

played if possible."

Arranging the dedication ceremony took a great deal of diplomacy on Gathman's part as he recalled in a 1984 interview.

"The United Auto Workers felt they should have their say and I agreed. The state had some ideas." As Gathman worked to satisfy both sides, some of the plans city officials had for the dedication were discarded.

"A lot of our ideas were bypassed," Gathman said.

During the week before the April 19, 1959 dedication, city workers poured gravel on the unpaved edges of blacktopped streets and swept the side streets alongside the street where the home was located, which now as a result of council action had been rechristened Truman Street.

American flags were placed on light poles and signs welcoming Truman were placed prominently throughout the route he would be taking and where visitors would be able to see them.

A welcoming committee including Gerald Gilkey was appointed to greet the former president when he arrived. The dedication was taking place two days before Gilkey officially joined the City Council.

Mayor Gathman and Bud Moore arranged a speaker's stand for the dedication ceremony with Lamar School District Superintendent Ted Windes arranging for the school's public address system to be moved to the Birthplace.

The *Lamar Democrat* office was set up as a media center with Luanna Aull, Madeleine Aull VanHafften and Stan and Betty White serving as hosts.

Though there would be no live national radio or television broadcasts of the event, network reporters were there, as once again were representatives of the wire services and the *New York Times*.

Reporters from the Kansas City, St. Louis and Springfield newspapers crowded into the *Democrat* office, as well as their counterparts with the *Joplin Globe* and *Joplin News-Herald*.

Marvin VanGilder and photographer Gene Smith represented the *Carthage Evening Press*. Since the *Democrat* rarely used photos, the Press had agreed to share Smith's photos.

City officials were concerned about the weather when it rained the previous evening and the skies were still cloud-covered the morning of April 19, but barring problems with the weather, the City of Lamar was ready to once again enjoy the spotlight.

Everything was ready for Harry Truman's return.

CHAPTER THIRTY-SIX

—— ∞ ——

The Plaza Theatre on the south side of the Lamar square was notable for being the first fully air conditioned building in Barton County when A. J. "Simmy" Simmons began operating it in the 1930s, at the height of the Depression.

Simmons invested heavily in the business as Marvin Van-Gilder recalled years later.

At a time when many other business executives in the district were guarding their dwindling resources with nervous intensity, (Simmons) and associates courageously invested in an ultra-modern theater adorned with the glow of prosperity, gambling that the bright beauty and positive symbolism would stimulate spending and recapture the progressive attitude that had been wiped out by the depressed national economy.

Simmons' gamble paid off almost immediately as he ran first-run features, often at the same time they were appearing in theaters in Denver and Chicago.

To a young VanGilder, who plunked down his nickels for whenever he was able to sell enough rabbits and pos- es from his trap lines, the Plaza Theater was a welcome from the daunting prospect of reality.

The highlight for many Lamar residents for the first quarter of a century of the Plaza's existence was the Sunday matinee.

After church services and the Sunday meal, families often watched a movie at the Plaza.

The matinee had been a staple of Lamar life for 25 years, but on Sunday, April 19, 1959, the Plaza Theatre went dark as the current owner, Harley Fryer, along with the rest of the community awaited Truman's arrival.

Restaurants and drugstores remained open so out-of-town visitors would be able to have a meal or soft drinks. It was the first day of Lamar's status as a tourist attraction.

The unusual spectacle of seven covered wagons drawn by horses and Missouri mules greeted the more than 1,000 people who gathered on the square in Independence the morning of April 19.

Wagon master Gordon "Tex" Serpa, who bore a strong resemblance to Roy Rogers, the star of dozens of movie westerns, was leading a caravan consisting of 21 Oregon residents, a dozen men, six women and three children, all dressed in 1840s style on a 2,000 mile trek from Independence, Missouri to Independence, Oregon as part of the State of Oregon's centennial celebration.

The trip was officially known as the On to Oregon Cavalcade.

A few moments before the long journey began, Serpa and those who were with him in the lead wagon talked with the honorary wagon master, someone who knew his way around Missouri mules.

He wished them well and as the barricade was lifted so the wagons could leave, Harry S. Truman called out, Westward ho! God bless you! Let her go!"

It was the beginning of what promised to be a long day for the former president.

Originally, Bess had been scheduled to make the trip to Lamar, but she was not feeling well and decided to remain in Independence.

Shortly after the wagon train departed, Truman left for Lamar. There was no limousine or chauffeured automobile to take him to Barton County.

It was years before Secret Service protection was authorized for former presidents.

Harry Truman drove from Independence to Lamar. He arrived in the city at 11:30 a.m. earlier than expected, surprising the welcoming committee and various state officials and dignitaries at the Travelers Hotel.

The Chancellor family sold the hotel in 1952 to the Henson Corporation, which just one year later sold it to the Foster sisters, Versah and Letha and their mother, Myrtle.

The owners had worked furiously to prepare the hotel for the Truman festivities. Realizing that the banquet hall would be inadequate for the number of people that were expected, extra tables were brought in.

The Travelers had also been designated as the contingency plan in case rain prevented the dedication ceremony from being held at the Birthplace so the hotel had to be prepared for that possibility.

By the time Truman reached the Lamar city limits, the sun was shining, but clouds kept ominously appearing every few minutes.

Harry Truman examines the monument in front of the Truman Birth-place. *Photo courtesy of Truman Library and Museum*

From the Travelers Hotel, Truman made his first visit to the house where he was born since his return to Lamar in 1944.

Joseph Jaeger, Jr., state parks director, showed him the improvements that had been made to the house and Truman expressed his approval, adding, "It looks a little different than I remember it."

In one bedroom, two photos on the wall captured Truman's attention- one was of him as a baby, the other a picture of Martha Truman.

Truman's next stop was the home of an old friend, Harriet Spradling, for a private buffet luncheon in the dining room and on the patio.

Harry S. Truman at the dedication of the Truman Birthplace April 19, 1959. *Photos courtesy of Truman Library and Museum*

Harry S. Truman at the dedication of the Truman Birthplace April 19, 1959. *Photos courtesy of Truman Library and Museum*

Crowds gather at the dedication of the Truman Birthplace April 19, 1959.

Photos courtesy of Truman Library and Museum

Crowds gather at the dedication of the Truman Birthplace April 19, 1959.

Photos courtesy of Truman Library and Museum

Harry S. Truman at the dedication of the Truman Birthplace April 19, 1959. *Photo courtesy of Truman Library and Museum*

From 1 to 3:30 p.m., a reception honoring Truman's old Army unit, Battery D, was held at Memorial Hall.

As the reception neared its conclusion, the crowd, which was later estimated at around 7,000 people, began to gather at the Truman home in anticipation of the dedication ceremony.

Shortly after 3:30, a parade, led by the Lamar High School Band and the 35th Division Missouri National Guard Band, started at the square and made the four-block trek to the Truman house.

Truman, whose morning routine in Independence always included a walk through his neighborhood, kept up with the bands' brisk pace, as he walked behind them.

Lamar residents and out-of-town visitors stood side-by-side

Crowds gather at the dedication of the Truman Birthplace April 19, 1959.
Photo courtesy of Truman Library and Museum

Harry S. Truman walks in the parade during the dedication of the Truman Birthplace April 19, 1959. *Photo courtesy of Truman Library and Museum*

the entire length of the parade route cheering constantly as Truman passed.

The smile never left the former president's face as he waved his hat at the crowds and stopped every once in a while to talk to someone, usually a child.

Randall Jessee, director of the Metropolitan Area Planning Council in Kansas City, served as master of ceremonies, introducing United Auto Workers Vice President Leonard Woodcock, who substituted for President Walter Reuther, who was unable to be in Lamar due to a throat infection.

Woodcock officially presented the deed to the Truman house to Missouri Gov. James Blair, who promised the state would "preserve this site as a show place for all the world.

"The men and women of the United Auto Workers, led by their gifted president make this gift because they believe in what President Truman stood for in his public career.

"We in Missouri accept it with pleasure because President Truman, by his life and works, has become the number one citizen of our state."

A highlight of the ceremony followed as 17-year-old Donald Braker, president of the Lamar High School Student Council, stepped to the microphone to present Truman with a plaque from the people of Lamar.

Braker's dark suit was accentuated by a white carnation on his lapel. If the teenager was nervous, he showed no sign of it. Public speaking was nothing new for Braker.

Only two days earlier at the Missouri FFA Convention, Braker had captured first place in oratory.

Braker turned to Truman and said, "You are symbolic of every American boy's secret ambition.'

He held the bronze plaque and noted it would be displayed

Harry S. Truman walks in the parade during the dedication of the Truman Birthplace April 19, 1959. *Photos courtesy of Truman Library and Museum*

prominently in the house in the room where a future president had been born on May 8, 1884 to offer "vivid proof that wealth and pretentious surroundings aren't necessary for greatness."

Braker read the inscription.

President Truman with Lamar High School Student Council President Donald Braker at the Truman Birthplace Dedication Ceremony. *Photo courtesy of Barton County Historical Society*

In this room on May 8, 1884, was born President Harry S. Truman whose faith in the youth of this country has been an inspiration to all. In honest and sincere appreciation- The Citizens of Lamar

Braker concluded by again turning to the former president

and saying, "Lamar is proud of you, its native son."

Truman shook hands with Braker, posed for several photos and said, "You'd better look out for that boy because Missouri may have another occupant in the White House some day."

Jessee introduced Sen. Symington for the dedicatory address.

Starting today, people will come to Lamar from all over the world. They will be making the pilgrimage to learn about the beginnings of this man of Missouri who wrote for himself an imperishable chapter in history.

They will see that what went into the making of Harry Truman was America itself.

Symington stressed that Truman's life would be noteworthy even if he had never become president "because his life and character have been a mirror of America."

Symington detailed Truman's humble beginning and the early obstacles to his success when he struggled as a small business owner and how he rose above those struggles to reach high office.

"On April 12, 1945, Harry S. Truman did become president and what he did for the next seven years will be remembered as long as free men walk the earth."

The final speaker was the one thousands had waited to see. Truman still looking dapper in a navy blue suit that remained unwrinkled despite the full schedule he had followed since serving as honorary wagon master for the caravan leaving Independence that morning, looked out over the crowd taking in the scene before he spoke.

Truman was especially gratified to see the number of small children in the audience. From his vantage point, he could see some had squeezed to the front. Others such as the five-year-

Harry S. Truman at the dedication of the Truman Birthplace April 19, 1959. *Photos courtesy of Truman Library and Museum*

Harry S. Truman at the dedication of the Truman Birthplace April 19, 1959. *Photos courtesy of Truman Library and Museum*

old boy whose father carried him on his shoulders so he could watch as history unfolded, found different ways to take in the event.

Lamar's most famous native son thanked its citizens, the people of the United Auto Workers and everyone else who came to the home on Truman Avenue.

They don't do this for a former president until he's been dead 50 years. I feel like I've been buried and dug up while I'm still alive and I'm glad they've done it to me today.

I am overwhelmed by this immense outpouring of Missourians and people from neighboring states. You don't know how I appreciate all this. I'm extremely touched.

When the ceremony concluded, more than 2,000 people

Harry Truman thanked the people of Missouri during the dedication of his birthplace. *Photo courtesy of Truman Library and Museum*

The United Auto Workers held a dinner in President Truman's honor at the Travelers Hotel following the birthplace dedication ceremony. *Photo courtesy of Truman Library and Museum*

lined up to tour the house with the first visitor being the person who had been born in a small bedroom there almost 75 years earlier.

The former President of the United States and U. S. senator from the State of Missouri signed his name to the register– "Harry Truman, Independence, Mo. Retired Farmer."

Truman talked with people outside the House for a while before he made a second trip to the Harriett Spradling home, where he rested before the next activities began.

The last stop on Truman's itinerary was the Travelers Hotel where the United Auto Workers gave a dinner in his honor with 240 people attending.

The Travelers staff provided a meal that consisted of cold

Harry S. Truman at the dedication of the Truman Birthplace April 19, 1959. *Photos courtesy of Truman Library and Museum*

Harry S. Truman at the dedication of the Truman Birthplace April 19, 1959. *Photos courtesy of Truman Library and Museum*

sliced turkey, fried chicken, mashed potatoes, gravy, green beans, spring salad, hot rolls, butter, jelly and relishes with a strawberry chiffon pie and coffee for dessert.

The Travelers Hotel was filled with laughter as Truman thoroughly enjoyed the company of a room filled with friends.

After saying his goodbyes, Truman was back in his car and on the way home to Independence.

Sunday, April 19, 1959, Lamar showed its appreciation for Harry Truman. It was his last visit to the city where he was born.

CHAPTER THIRTY-SEVEN

Former Mayor Loyd Gathman offered a tempting business proposal to Gerald Gilkey in 1960.

Gathman, who owned the Chevrolet dealership in Lamar, approached Gilkey about buying his business. Though having his own dealership was something Gilkey dearly wanted, he rejected Gathman's proposal because he felt it would be disloyal to the Medlin family. He was not going into competition against his own family.

The offer started Gilkey thinking about buying a dealership away from Lamar and when he learned of an opportunity to buy a dealership in Abilene, Kansas, he jumped on it and was working on the details of the purchase with the owners.

It was a difficult decision. In the 10 years Gilkey had lived in Lamar he had grown to love the city. He enjoyed the people, the sense of community and the feeling that he was contributing through his work on the City Council.

He and Betty weighed the pros and cons of making the move. They would be moving away from their families and taking their son Steve out of his school and away from his friends, but this was what Gilkey had dreamed of doing almost since his first day in the auto sales business and they decided to pull the trigger and make the move to Abilene.

When Betty's brother Jewell Medlin learned what his brother-in-law was planning, he made a counteroffer- He would sell his dealership to Gilkey,

It was the perfect solution. Gilkey, who was two months into his second term on the Lamar City Council, gratefully accepted the offer.

He contacted Gathman and closed a deal to buy the Chevrolet dealership and Gilkey Chevrolet opened at 902 Broadway.

In July 1961, Gerald Gilkey became the owner of the Chevrolet and Oldsmobile franchises for Lamar.

Nine-year-old Paula VanGilder was the youngest member of the press corps registered to cover the festivities surrounding Thomas Hart Benton Day in Neosho Sunday, May 12, 1962, the day the 73-year-old Benton, one of the foremost artists in the nation, returned for the first time in 50 years.

Benton and his wife Rita arrived on a special Kansas City Southern train from Kansas City with 100 others, including the artist's best friend, Harry Truman and Bess.

They were greeted at the station by the local National Guard unit and the Neosho High School Band and were cheered by thousands during a brief parade around the Neosho Square. Benton and his wife sat in the first car, while Truman, making a conscious effort not to upstage Benton on his special day, rode with Bess in the fifth car in the parade, an open-top convertible.

The parade stopped at the Neosho Municipal Auditorium

where Truman unveiled a specially commissioned portrait of Benton done by Miami, Oklahoma artist Charles Banks Wilson.

"It is a great honor for me, a Missourian, to unveil this portrait of Mr. Benton, who is the greatest artist of the century."

After the portrait's unveiling, Benton accepted Truman's praise with humility.

"I'm not exactly accepting that," Benton said. "I can, however, accept that from the President of the United States, but the proposition is debatable."

During a press conference, some reporters tossed questions at Truman, who was having none of it.

"I've had a thousand press conferences. This is Tom's show."

Truman brushed aside one political question by joking, "I don't think I'd better talk about that. This is Republican country."

Marvin VanGilder, representing the *Carthage Press*, introduced his daughter Paula to the former president, jokingly adding that she was a Republican.

Truman proceeded to win that Republican's support with the heartfelt charm offensive that always accompanied his dealings with children.

He made sure to have Paula in photos with him and as Marvin VanGilder recalled years later, "(He) stooped a bit from his usual military erect posture to make certain she was not left out of the resulting pictures."

For VanGilder, who had loved history since his childhood, the opportunity to be in the same room with Harry S. Truman, with whom he had corresponded since first contacting him about the formation of a Barton County Historical Society years earlier, and Thomas Hart Benton, was an experience he would never forget.

The kindness Truman showed his daughter further cemented VanGilder's belief that the former president was that rarity, a Democrat he could admire.

A highlight of the annual American Royal Livestock and Horse Show October 16, 1963 in Kansas City was the return after an eight-year absence of Missouri mules.

To the delight of the crowd of 6,500, the judge for the show, Harry S. Truman, entered the arena in a wagon drawn by four sorrel mules.

Truman told reporters that evening, "The best mules I ever drove were six gray mules that belonged to my uncle. I remember the lead pair were named Pearl and Fanny."

The first place winner among the nine mules entered in the competition was a two-year-old named Jane, owned by the same man who drove him into the arena, Claude "Brother" Adams of Lamar, whose mules had made a fine showing in the inaugural parade 14 years earlier.

The win did not surprise Brother Adams.

After all, he had always known that Harry Truman knew something about mules.

In 1965, after serving six years as Lamar mayor, Norbert Heim elected not to run for a fourth two-year term and asked Gerald Gilkey to consider running for the office.

Gilkey had done more than just attend council meetings

and vote. He had thrived on committee work and had a knack for smoothing over disagreements and solving problems.

In April 1965, Gilkey was elected mayor and from the beginning, it became apparent that Heim had a made a wise selection.

Each day as the years passed, Lamar residents with problems made their way to Gilkey Chevrolet to seek help from the mayor or to express their anger at something that was happening in the city.

"We had people come in mad, slamming doors when they went into his office," his granddaughter, Courtney Gardner, said, "but by the time they came out they were laughing and best friends."

Gilkey's son Steve, who worked at the car dealership with his father, said there was an initial fear that Gilkey being mayor would have an adverse effect on the business, but it never did.

"He had a way with people. They'd get mad at him as mayor, but not the person. They would keep doing business with him. I don't know how he did that."

The job occasionally crept into Gilkey's home life, as well.

"He would get calls at night and he would talk to them," his wife Betty recalled. "I just would not have had that patience."

Steve Gilkey remembered, "There was one lady who would call and say she had UFOs outside her window and ask him to send the police department down there."

With that woman, as well as anyone else who called, Gilkey always listened and even when the person who called did not get the results he or she had hoped for, things seemed better when the call ended.

OO

Since the April 19, 1959 dedication of the Truman Birthplace, its status as a tourist attraction for the City of Lamar had continued to grow, but at times it seemed that it was not a high priority for the State of Missouri.

The administration of the birthplace had been placed in the hands of Truman's old friend Harriet Spradling, but as the '60s were coming to a close, with Spradling reaching age 75, past state retirement age, the management of the historic site became haphazard.

Recognizing the problem and realizing it was time for a change in management, though the state was not prepared to put in a veteran well-trained administrator, a call came from Jefferson City to a man who knew the City of Lamar and had a knack for recognizing and encouraging those with ability, something he had developed from his time serving in the U. S. Army Air Force during the second world war.

Sure enough, Richard Chancellor, who had moved into banking after the closing of the Lawn Boy plant and was president of Barton County State Bank, knew just the person for the job.

Jim Finley, a Lamar native, returned to the city in 1968 after serving more than two decades in the U. S. Air Force, a time span that included service in World War II, the Korean Conflict and the Vietnam War.

At first, he tried at his hand at farming, but it became clear quickly that this was not what he wanted to do with the rest of his life.

"He didn't like the cows," his wife Nell said.

Finley took a job at Thorco Industries and that was where he was working when Chancellor approached him about the position.

Finley was interested in the position as Truman Birthplace administrator and was hired.

Finley enjoyed taking care of the house and the grounds and managing the budget, but more than anything he enjoyed the people who came to see the house where Harry Truman was born.

Many of those who came to Lamar had served during World War II and were grateful to Truman for bringing the war to an end.

"He really did like talking to those old soldiers," Nell Finley said. "That was the thing he really loved about his job."

CHAPTER THIRTY-EIGHT

An era in community journalism ended on November 1, 1972 when Madeleine announced in a page one article that after 72 years, the Aull family was selling the *Lamar Democrat*.

Arthur Aull's widow, Luanna, died in 1968 at age 95 and there were no younger family members to continue the tradition. Madeleine had divorced Carl VanHafften more than 20 years earlier, following the Aull tradition of telling the entire story on page one of the newspaper. The couple had no children and Madeleine was 74.

Stan and Betty White also had no children.

Neither Genevieve Turrentine, Arthur Aull's third daughter, nor her children had any desire to run the *Democrat*.

Despite that, they had not planned to sell the newspaper until they were approached by Missouri Secretary of State James Kirkpatrick, who in addition to being a politician was in the newspaper business, having served as editor at the *Warrensburg Daily Star-Journal* and the *Jefferson City News Tribune* and later owning the *Windsor Review*.

Madeleine and Stan White realized that the style of newspaper they were publishing was outdated and they had no appetite for any major changes.

"We had to sell," Madeleine said. "The revolution of offset printing is with us and at our age, it isn't wise to take on such a change.

"That's for young men like Don Kirkpatrick," she added, referring to Kirkpatrick's son who became publisher after the sale was finalized.

In her final article for the *Democrat* after 26 years as editor, Madeleine wrote a heartfelt goodbye to readers.

It is with a feeling more poignant than regret, rather akin to sorrow that we relinquish the editorship of the paper.

But there comes a time in every life when sentiment must yield to stern reality. That time has arrived for us.

And so we say, "Hail and farewell" to the Democrat.

Madeleine told Marvin VanGilder she planned to do some creative writing, something she had never been able to do while filling the columns of a newspaper every day.

As the Kirkpatricks took control of the newspaper, there was a sadness to those who had loyally worked for the Aulls.

"I don't remember Madeleine ever coming back to the *Democrat* office," long time typesetter Dorothy Parks said.

The newspaper that had been her entire existence was no longer a part of her life and it was difficult for Madeleine to adjust.

"I have been at loose ends since the sale," she told a *St. Louis Post-Dispatch* reporter six weeks after the sale. "It was a traumatic experience. One of my difficulties will be keeping myself occupied."

When the next major story to hit Lamar came on December 26, 1972, a story that would certainly have brought out Madeleine's touch for the poetic, someone else was writing it.

It was left to the new owners of the *Democrat* to tell their readers that Harry Truman, the man who rose from humble beginnings in a small frame house on Kentucky Avenue in Lamar, had died in Independence at age 88.

CHAPTER THIRTY-NINE

"Death Finally Defeats Truman" was the banner headline at the top of the Tuesday, December 26, 1972 *Democrat*.

Lamar and the nation are in mourning for the city's native son, Harry S. Truman, 32nd President of the United States.

The former president died at 7:30 a.m. Tuesday after a long illness brought on by old age. The famed Missouri Democrat was 88 years old and fought his last illness as fiercely as he fought all his life for what he believed was right.

His wife Bess was not at his bedside when death came, but was notified several minutes afterwards. She had stayed at his side throughout Christmas Day, leaving only when the couple's daughter, Margaret Truman Daniel, arrived in Kansas City.

Truman's death was the subject of three more page one articles in the *Democrat* that day. One recalled his August 31, 1944 visit while the other featured reminiscences of the April 19, 1959, Truman Birthplace dedication ceremony.

The 1944 article inaccurately stated that Truman left Lamar 18 months after his birth, rather than 10, and said he never returned until 1944, a visit that was actually at least his fourth since John and Martha Truman left the city.

Former Mayor Guy Ross was quoted in the 1944 article. There appeared to be no interviews with anyone for the 1959 article.

The fourth article was an assessment of Truman's career by James Kirkpatrick.

Lamar readers were left to wonder what Madeleine would have written about the death of Lamar's most famous native son.

Jim Finley placed a wreath at the base of the granite monument in front of the Truman house and closed the historic site at the direction of state officials Thursday, December 28.

Two hundred fifty people gathered on the south lawn of the Truman Birthplace for a memorial service.

"We are proud in Lamar of Harry S. Truman," Mayor Gerald Gilkey said. "There is no doubt he will go down in history as one of the greatest presidents of the United States."

Gilkey remembered the excitement in Lamar when Truman returned for the notification ceremony in 1944 and for the dedication of the birthplace in 1959 and closed his remarks with sentiments that were fervently echoed by those who listened to his words.

"It is with respect and affection that we say farewell to that man born in Lamar, the 33rd President of the United States, Harry S. Truman."

The most eloquent remembrance of Truman written by

someone from Lamar came not from the *Lamar Democrat*, but in the pages of the *Carthage Press*, where Marvin VanGilder, the one time teen reporter for the *Lamar Republican* and reporter and columnist for the *Lamar Journal*, wrote a tribute to the former president.

VanGilder did not make a habit of personalizing his reporting, but he made an exception for the Truman tribute, recalling some of the correspondence they exchanged over the years concerning Barton County history.

He shared the story of the kindness Truman had shown his nine-year-old daughter at the Thomas Hart Benton celebration in Neosho 10 years earlier, recalled ways in which Truman had helped the city of Carthage, then closed by putting into words the powerful connection Truman had with him and with the people of southwest Missouri.

In spite of differences in political philosophy, the writer will remember him as a cherished friend and confidant with a heart big enough to embrace the most famous and the least known with equal ardor and the soul of a historian whose every major act was the result of thorough knowledge of the lessons learned by his predecessors.

He was a big man, he who first was our neighbor, later our chosen leader and always our friend.

The world, which never knew him in quite the way we knew him, will forever remember him as man of strength and purpose who stood firmly in defense of human liberty and individual dignity and who exuberantly achieved his own goal and his own destiny by becoming a good and faithful servant of both the God he worshipped and the people he served.

CHAPTER FORTY

"My father gave me two pieces of advice. Tell everything and tell it just as if you were talking. Sometimes certain people were not pleased about the tell everything part."

It was the first time the public had seen words from Madeleine Aull VanHafften in writing since the sale of the *Democrat*.

"I believe a newspaper should be a mirror of the community in that it reflects exactly what goes on in the community, good or bad. No newspaper is going to have the confidence of a community if it plays favorites."

After the sale of the newspaper she loved, she lived quietly at the same house at 400 W. 11th Street where she had lived with Arthur and Luanna Aull for the previous 35 years, just a few blocks from the square and the *Democrat* office.

Madeleine's comments were part of an obituary printed in the *Springfield News-Leader* November 22, 1977. Madeleine died the previous day, one day after her 79th birthday.

Despite an intermittent rain throughout the day, the Truman Centennial celebration in Lamar May 5, 1984 was a success.

As the evening approached, much of the community and many from out of town, more than 1,500 total waited in the bleachers at the Lamar High School football field for the performance of the Truman Pageant.

Much of the material in the pageant script was based on two sources- the writings from Lee Chiswell's *Lamar Democrat* of 100 years earlier and the long-delayed, but well received, *Story of Barton County* by Marvin VanGilder.

VanGilder was among those in the audience who watched, with ominous rain clouds hovering overhead, as the Lamar of 1884 came alive with more than 100 townspeople playing their counterparts from a century earlier.

Tackling his role with the same enthusiasm that still characterized his job as mayor of Lamar after 19 years, Gerald Gilkey played mayor and clothing store owner N. E. McCutchen, waving a pair of long johns (the finest you could find) that his store had just received.

Lamar Democrat Publisher Doug Davis and attorney Edison Kaderly were cast as the original *Democrat* owners Lee Chiswell and C. W. Huggins.

Richard Chancellor was the banker M. N. Wills and Dr. Thomas Carroll played W. L. Griffin, the doctor who delivered the Truman baby.

There was never any doubt who would play the roles of mule trader John Truman and his wife Martha.

Claude Oscar Adams, who as a five-year-old had ridden on his father's mule-drawn wagon in the 1949 Presidential Inauguration Parade and his wife, Kay, played the Trumans.

As the pageant unfolded, the rain gradually starting coming down harder, but no one left the stadium. When the pageant reached its conclusion, the rains that had stayed away on the day that Harry Truman was born and during his visits to Lamar in 1944 and 1959 finally came down, drenching the performers and virtually destroying the recreation of the 1884 Lamar square.

But not until after Harry S. Truman was born.

Two months before the Truman Centennial, an advertisement was placed in the *Joplin Globe, Springfield News-Leader* and regional newspapers across the Midwest advertising the Travelers Hotel was for sale.

"Be part of a historic landmark," the ad in the March, 18, 1984, *Joplin Globe* read.

"A steal for $65,000."

The eventual purchaser had no intention of keeping the Travelers Hotel intact, historic landmark or not.

William Magers, Springfield, the owner of the First National Bank of Golden City, wanted to open a branch in Lamar to serve as the headquarters for both banking facilities.

After the sale was completed, a public auction was held December 27, 1984 at the hotel with those attending knowing that once the auction was completed, it would not be long before the building was razed to make room for a modern bank building with multiple drive-through lanes.

Over several hours every last remnant of the Travelers Hotel was sold- three Casablanca ceiling fans, an Evers and Pond upright piano and bench, a small scale antique stagecoach, a cast iron claw bathtub, a large antique safe, old light fixtures

The Travelers Hotel was torn down to make room for the First National Bank of Lamar in 1985. *Photo courtesy of Barton County Historical Society*

and even room keys.

Many who were not bidders came to look at the interior of the Travelers Hotel for a final time.

Among those who made the pilgrimage were Richard Chancellor, whose family had owned the hotel for 20 years, and Marvin VanGilder, who, as a teenager, had worked at the Travelers.

A month later, the Travelers Hotel, the place where history had been made and special moments created by the visits of Harry S. Truman, existed only in memory, another sacrifice at the altar of progress.

The contributions of Marvin VanGilder, whose career in journalism began in 1940 continued following his publication of *The Story of Barton County* in 1972. It was the first of many books VanGilder contributed, with a special emphasis on the

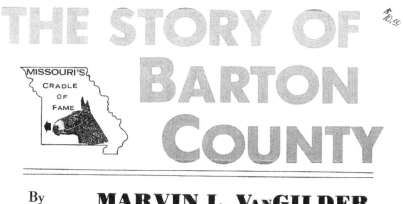

By **MARVIN L. VanGILDER**

The Story of Barton County by Marvin L. VanGilder was published in 1972.

Civil War history of Carthage and the surrounding area.

VanGilder was instrumental in the designation of the Battle of Carthage State Park and continued to instill in young journalists an appreciation of the history of the communities in which they served. His career as a full-time journalist, which included years serving as news director at KDMO Radio in Carthage and as managing editor of the *Carthage Press*, continued until 1993, when he retired.

Retirement, however, did not stop his prolific writing or his work at the *Press*. For the next several years, he continued to write a history column and a news column every week, as well as contributing unsigned editorials.

In August 1996, after 42 years away from writing for a Lamar newspaper, VanGilder once again found himself aligned with a newspaper that was challenging the firmly entrenched *Lamar Democrat*.

VanGilder wrote a weekly column on Lamar history for the *Lamar Press*, a weekly launched by the *Carthage Press*.

Forty-nine weeks later, the *Press*, like the *Lamar Journal* and *Lamar Republican* before it, published its last issue.

∞

One key to Gerald Gilkey's success as mayor of Lamar was the quality of the people working for him at his car dealership.

Gilkey was comfortable leaving his staff, which included son Steve, in charge while he represented Lamar's interests at regional meetings in Joplin and Springfield, in front of state officials in Jefferson City and even in Washington, D. C.

"It allowed Dad to do what he wanted to do," Steve Gilkey said. "He really loved politics.

Together with the City Council, Gilkey steered Lamar through the most successful period in its history. Through an advantageous deal for purchasing electricity, the city made enough money that in both 1983 and 1986, city residents received the holiday gift of no electric bills for the month of December.

The 1983 Christmas gift received national publicity from the wire services and through a mention on the nationally syndicated Paul Harvey radio show.

More national attention came to Gerald and Steve Gilkey the following year when Lamar became the first community in the nation in which the same owners operated both the Chevrolet and Ford dealerships.

Other successes for the City of Lamar while Gilkey was mayor included the area's first aquatic park, the construction of a performing arts auditorium and lobbying successfully along with council members, Nell Finley and State Representative Jerry Burch, to stop a state plan to cut the hours the Truman

Betty and Gerald Gilkey at a retirement reception in 2001 after Gilkey stepped down after 36 years as Lamar's mayor. *Photo courtesy of Gilkey family*

Birthplace remained open.

Every two years, like clockwork, Gilkey filed for re-election, serving as mayor for 36 years, the longest person to ever serve as a mayor in Missouri history. Counting his time on City Council, he served the City of Lamar for 42 years.

"He was never tempted to quit," Betty Gilkey said.

Gilkey's last council meeting was on April 16, 2001. When his final meeting adjourned, his successor as mayor, long time City Councilman Keith Divine, was sworn in and among the new council members, representing Ward One, the same position that Gilkey once held, was Steve Gilkey.

On July 17, 2006, one year after Gerald Gilkey's death, the Gilkey family attended a ceremony in the city's Thiebaud Auditorium unveiling a portrait of Lamar's long-time mayor.

Betty Gilkey at the Thiebaud Auditorium in Lamar in 2006 at an unveiling of a portrait of her husband Mayor Gerald Gilkey. *Photo by Randy Turner*

Mayor Keith Divine said the portrait captured the Gerald Gilkey he had served with for 23 years down to that "certain twinkle" in his eyes.

Divine announced the portrait would hang on the east wall of the Lamar City Hall lobby and that when and if a new city hall was ever built, it would be named after Gerald Gilkey.

Betty Gilkey told the more than 200 who attended the ceremony, "The city was his love. He loved all the people."

In 2019, the Gilkey family, Betty, Steve and his wife Nancy, and their three children Courtney Gardner, Katie Gilkey and John Gilkey, all remain in Lamar, with John serving on the Lamar City Council.

"He was happy that we all decided to stay here," Steve Gilkey said.

"Lamar has been good to us.' "

Kent Harris, 65, is in his third year as mayor of Lamar, a job he was elected to after succeeding Keith Divine, who served for 16 years after Gerald Gilkey stepped down.

Harris served 18 years on the City Council, working with both Gilkey and Divine, prior to his election as mayor and has lived in the city most of his life and in Barton County since he was born.

Despite the city and the Barton County Chamber of Commerce marketing Lamar's connections to Harry Truman and Wyatt Earp as "The City Where Legends Begin," Harris sees the knowledge of who Truman is and his importance is fading.

"That's happened as the older generation passed on," he said.

When Debbie (his wife) and I are traveling, we always make sure to tell people we are from Lamar and that we are from the birthplace of Harry Truman."

Lamar Mayor Kent Harris. *Photo Courtesy of City of Lamar*

That especially is meaningful to those the Harrises have met while traveling outside the U. S. borders.

"I mention Harry Truman and they know who he is."

Though Harris thinks many of the city's younger residents will gradually come to appreciate Truman as they grow older, he is aware that the generation that experienced Truman's impact on Lamar will no longer be around to share the memories of the excitement that Truman's visits generated.

Harris considers himself fortunate to be among those who saw Harry Truman when the former president came to Lamar. Though he has no recollection of what Truman said, he can picture it clearly.

Harris, five years old at the time, had an unobstructed view as he sat atop his father's shoulders the last time Truman came to Lamar.

ABOUT THE AUTHOR

Randy Turner, a Joplin, Missouri resident, is a retired English teacher.

Prior to his teaching career, Turner was a newspaper reporter and editor for 22 years, earning more than 30 national, regional and state awards for investigative reporting.

Recommended Reading

The following books were used as sources and/or provided valuable information:

Ferrell, Robert H. *Choosing Truman: The Democratic Convention of 1944*, University of Missouri Press 1994

Ferrell, Robert H (editor) *Dear Bess: The Letters from Harry to Bess Truman 1910-1959* W. W. Norton and Co. 1983

History of Hickory, Polk, Cedar, Dade and Barton Counties, Missouri The Printery 1889

McCulloch, David *Truman* Simon & Schuster 1992

Miller, Merle *Plain Speaking: An Oral Biography of Harry S. Truman* Berkley Publishing Group 1974

Stebbins, Chad *All the News is Fit to Print: Profile of a Country Editor* University of Missouri Press 1998

Tefertiller, Casey *Wyatt Earp: The Life Behind the Legend* John Wiley and Sons, Inc. 1998

Truman, Harry S. *Year of Decision: Memoirs by Harry S. Truman* Time, Inc. 1955

Truman, Margaret *Bess W. Truman* MacMillan Publishing Co. 1986

Truman, Margaret, *Harry S. Truman* William Morrow & Co. 1973

VanGilder, Marvin L. *The Story of Barton County* 1972

Young, Reba Earp *Down Memory Lane* 1993

Made in the USA
Coppell, TX
29 November 2020